Swing Trading

A Beginner's Guide to Highly Profitable Swing Trades - Proven Strategies, Trading Tools, Rules, and Money Management

By

Mark Lowe

© Copyright 2018 - All rights reserved.

The content contained within this book may not be reproduced, duplicated or transmitted without direct written permission from the author or the publisher.

Under no circumstances will any blame or legal responsibility be held against the publisher, or author, for any damages, reparation, or monetary loss due to the information contained within this book. Either directly or indirectly.

Legal Notice:

This book is copyright protected. This book is only for personal use. You cannot amend, distribute, sell, use, quote or paraphrase any part, or the content within this book, without the consent of the author or publisher.

Disclaimer Notice:

Please note the information contained within this document is for educational and entertainment purposes only. All effort has been executed to present accurate, up to date, and reliable, complete information. No warranties of any kind are declared or implied. Readers acknowledge that the author is not engaging in the rendering of legal, financial, medical or professional advice. The content within this book has been derived from various sources. Please consult a licensed professional before attempting any techniques outlined in this book.

By reading this document, the reader agrees that under no circumstances is the author responsible for any losses, direct or indirect, which are incurred as a result of the use of information contained within this document, including, but not limited to, — errors, omissions, or inaccuracies.

Table of Contents

Introduction 5

Chapter 1 – An Introduction to Financial Trading 8

    What are the Basics of Financial Trading? 8

Chapter 2 - What is Swing Trading? 27

    Introduction to Swing Trading 27

Chapter 3 - Finding a suitable Market 40

    Selecting a Financial Instrument to trade 40

Chapter 4 – Learning the Art of Swing Trading 67

    Learning the Art or Science of Swing Trading 67

Chapter 5 - The Art of Selling Short 76

    What is selling short all about? 76

Chapter 6 - The Basics of Fundamentals Analysis 84

    An introduction to Fundamental Analysis 84

Chapter 7 - The Basics of Technical Analysis 95

    What is Technical Analysis? 96

Chapter 8 - Designing a Swing Trade Strategy 113

    Devising a Swing Trading Strategy 114

Chapter 9 - Managing Risk 123

    Proper Position Size 123

Chapter 10 – Wrapping it all Up 134

Thank you! 138

Introduction

Swing trading is about taking a short-term position in the market whereby you identify recurring patterns in a stock price line, and then use that to your advantage to ride the wave and make a profit. It can be described best as the middle ground between the highly hectic and stressful world of day trading and the much more academic and studious approach of position trading. It can be said to be the best of both worlds as you don't have the stress of making a quick decision as you have the time to think things through. You can, for example, look at the recent data to see if you are trading on the correct side of the market, which is always a good thing. But as you also don't have the time and resources available to the position trader you do not get too caught up in your research which can lead to procrastination. Whereby the more you study a company's stock, the more confusing it becomes as you are trying to make sense of conflicting indicators which leads to analysis paralysis.

In swing trading, however, you are working on positions that last more than a day but in most likelihood less than a week, as you should focus on only one leg of a swing. That means you have the luxury of time to research and hone your strategy but not too much time to over think things.

Swing trading is, therefore, for many, a happy medium between day and position trading where you do have the opportunity to research and make informed decisions, but at the same time, you are looking for quick entry and exit points within a trade that makes you a profit on that price swing. After all, this is the core principle of swing trading; you study a trend then find a good low-price entry point, and then you ride the wave till the crest and quickly exit pocketing the profits.

Swing trading, however, is not easy, it requires that if you want to be successful that you perform diligent research and use wisely the subsequent knowledge you have discovered. This information is found through your fundamental and technical analysis – it is your analysis of the fundamentals of the company that makes you want to trade their stock, but it is the technical analysis that lets you manage and safely exit a trade. Establishing a careful strategy that takes into account, not just making profits, but by importantly managing potential losses. Never lose sight of the fact that wise account management and preservation of your capital is what will keep you in the game. Therefore, in this book, we strive to provide you with good advice and best practices that will enable you to build a sensible strategy that enables you to stay on the right side of the market.

With these good intentions in mind, we will give you, through the course of this book, profound advice on trading strategies, capital preservation, risk management, and position sizing. But it is not all doom and gloom because we will also show you how to identify emerging high-performing stocks and when and where to enter and exit a trade so that you optimize your profits. We will also show you how to lock-in your profits while you continue to ride the wave to even greater profits.

Swing Trading is by no means easy, but if you follow the advice in this book you will firmly have put the odds on your side, you will be confident in trading with the correct strategy in the market as well as in balancing your risk and reward dilemma - and you can't really ask for more than that.

Chapter 1 – An Introduction to Financial Trading

What are the Basics of Financial Trading?

In this introductory chapter, we will aim at getting you acquainted with the way the financial markets work and get you familiar with some of the terms and phrases that are commonly used in financial trading. If you are an outright beginner, you should read this chapter, or you may find later references to things like stock-loss orders or financial instruments too confusing. However, for those readers who are well acquainted with financial trading, you can skip this chapter.

There was a time when trading in what is called financial instruments – stocks, futures, options, and currencies - was an activity for only the wealthy. However, in recent years the financial markets have been transformed into platforms of wealth generation for many segments of the population. This has come about through the advances in data communications, trading technology as well as the advent of low-cost online stock brokerage services. These technological improvements have enabled the financial markets to open up to anyone with sufficient capital that wishes to buy or sell futures, options or shares.

However, although the stock market has opened up and technology has revolutionized the trading methods the underpinning core principles, and fundamentals remain. Therefore the market exists as a place for shares to be bought or sold for investment or speculation. Investing is done with the expectation that in the future, the company's stock will be worth more than the original investment. This does not mean that it is altruistic far from it as it is meant to be an informed decision made with full expectations of future profits - for you. When you invest, your money is meant to be put to work by the company to increase the stock value that can be realized as profit for you at a future time.

Speculation, on the other hand, is more like gambling. Speculators will buy stock with the hope that they can soon sell it at a higher price. This creates liquidity in the market. However, an important distinction between investors and speculators is that investors are generally more informed about the processes that create the underlying value as they are in it for the long haul. Speculators, on the other hand, are more interested in the price itself and in the shortest time for realizing a profit.

How are Stocks traded?

When a company decides to go public, it makes its shares available to public investors who can then trade them with other investors. Traditionally these shares were traded on the trading floor in a stock exchange such as the New York and London Stock Exchanges. However, the trend today for the low-volume, low value, retail traders is to move to virtual trading platforms hosted on the internet where trades transactions occur online over high-speed connections and each transaction is recorded electronically. This type of trading is referred to as over-the-counter trading.

However, regardless of whether the trading market is real or virtual, they are still considered to be secondary markets. This is because the trade of a company's stock is being conducted without the participation of the company. The market is, therefore, a meeting place – physical or virtual - where those wishing to sell their shares can find potential buyers. It is important to understand the underlying concept here that when you buy shares on the stock market, it is not the company that sells you the shares. Your money is not going back to the company. For the company has already sold those shares to the present shareholders. Instead, you are buying the share from some existing shareholders that are willing to sell. Likewise, when it comes your time to sell it is not the company or your broker that is buying them – it is to other

Investors who are in the market to buy. This is important to realize as often will be the case in a sudden price downtrend sellers will outweigh buyers. In this case, going by the basic rules of supply and demand prices must drop to a level where a buyer can be found and in a falling market finding a buyer may not always be easy.

Today, many stock exchanges around the world are linked together via high speed private fiber-optic communications links to facilitate speedy and efficient trading. These traditional exchanges are heavily regulated to ensure fair play and fair pricing. However, with the rise of the internet a new style of the virtual stock market has come about, and these may be more loosely regulated. These virtual markets are termed over-the-counter exchanges. Although most of these are reputable virtual exchanges more akin to bulletin boards their shares can be considered a higher risk. This is because the over-the-counter exchanges often do not demand or enforce the stricter criteria for listing of stock that the bigger traditional exchanges insist upon. For example, traditional exchanges will often require that a company meets certain conditions regarding company value, profitability and that it has been in business for a certain minimum number of years.

The traditional exchanges will do this to protect their reputation and their clients from rogue companies with often zero assets issuing frankly worthless shares.

The trading of shares on a stock market is typically through an auction process where buyers bid and sellers make offers. When there is a match between a bid and an offer a trade is made. Hence, a market consists of the bid to buy and an offer to sell, which is often referred to as an 'ask.' The buyer is making a bid at the price he wishes to buy at, and the seller is offering the price they wish to sell. The range of difference around the bid and offer prices is called the spread. The narrower the price spread and the larger the number of unmatched bids and offers then the larger the liquidity of the stock. Additionally, if there are many open (unmatched) buyers bids and sellers offers (asks) at a good range of prices, then this provides good depth. A general characteristic of good stock markets and also good shares is that they will tend to have small spreads, high liquidity, and good depth.

Many investors do not deal in individual company shares; instead, they are interested in current stock indexes. These are the aggregate prices of a selection of a variety of stocks. The movement of an index is the net effect of the individual price movement of each of the stocks in the group. For example, the S&P 500 is a market index of the 500 largest companies in the

U.S. However some indices can be specific to certain market sectors such as technology firms.

Finding a Brokerage

Historically, share trading was performed by licensed brokerage firms or brokers who make the actual trade on behalf of their clients typically through their traders buying or selling the stock on the open outcry trading floors of the major exchanges. The clients would typically be wealthy individuals that wished to play the market and trade in shares. Today, the bedlam of the open outcry trading floor is a thing of the past replaced by high-speed trading platforms that have brought an element of detachment from the trading mechanics but does little to relieve the analyst's stress levels.

Technology advances have brought about a wide selection of real or virtual brokerage services offering competitive trading commissions and transaction rates. However, the traditional brokerage service once only available to VIP clients still exists today. These concierge-style services are still targeted at the wealthy investor and take the form of a "full-service" whereby the broker offers for a fee, research, expert analysis, and advice tailored to the VIP client's requirements. However, for the traders with only limited funds, there are now many online brokerages that offer discount services by executing the trades.

As the adage goes, you get what you are willing to pay for and so it is with selecting a brokerage. So you are well advised to shop

Around, for a broker with the advent of electronic trading. Many online brokerages, as well as executing traders, are offering some level of research and opinion at low commissions that will suit the most budget-conscious beginner.

Buying and Selling Stock

The actual mechanics of trading shares is the same around the world regardless of the type of broker you use. The first step is to get a stock quote. There is a wealth of information within a stock quote. For example, there will be included along with the current highest bid and lowest offer (ask) prices it also tells you of the last price that was traded. Moreover, there will also be information on the number of shares being traded which is referred to as a volume. If the stock quotes are obtained online, they are often based on real-time data. Online quotes also often include attached charts and additional historical share trading data.

Stocks quotes are identified by using a device called a 'ticker symbol.' This is a representation or abbreviation of the company's name using between one or more, usually up to five, capital letters. For example, the ticker symbol for Facebook is FB, Apple is AAPL, and Alphabet's Google ticker is GOOG or GOOGL depending on the type of stock you want to buy.

Types of Orders

After you receive the stock quote and it has been duly analyzed the next step is to determine the type of trade you wish to make. This is done via one of two main methods – albeit there are other less common types of order, but for now, we will stick with the two main types. The two types of order that you must be aware of are, market orders and limited orders. The former will strive to fulfill your order for the number of shares at the lowest available price. The latter will only fulfill your order for available shares at the price you stipulate. To understand the difference and how this can affect you in practice let us take a closer look into how the market order works.

Market Orders

In this scenario, you want to buy 100 shares of Facebook at the best market price. On receiving the stock quote the price shows the following:
Bid: $139.80 (100), Offer: $140. (50), Last: $139.95 (250).
What this tells us is that the last shares traded were sold as a lot of 250 shares at a price of $139.95 and it also indicates that there are currently only 50 shares on offer at the currently available lowest price of $140. But our market order is for 100 shares.

Now if we consider that along comes another trader who then places 100 Facebook shares onto the market at an asking price of $140.05 now your market order would buy the 50 shares at $140. And go onto purchase 50 more at the next best price of $140.05.

That is the unique behavior of a market order that we need to understand. It will try to fulfill the order at the lowest available price. The focus is on getting the number of shares that you ordered but perhaps not at the price you wanted. Therefore, you should only use a market order when you are more concerned with getting hold of the number of shares rather than getting a certain price.

Limit Orders

On the other hand a limit order specifies the actual price at which you want the order fulfilled, but of course, that does not guarantee the order will be filled. When an order is completed it is said to be filled. For example, similar to the previous scenario if you make a limit order with a bid to buy 100 Facebook shares but this time for exactly $140. In this case, you would instead of using a market order you would issue a limit order limit order. This type of order when executed would immediately buy the 50 Facebook shares offered at $140. But then you would be unable to This means you would have to buy any more as none are on offer at your bid price.

Wait for the price to come down to match your buying price. Until this happens, the new quote would be:
Bid: $140. (50), Offer: $140.05 (200), Last: $140. (50).

With a limit order, you will guarantee the price is what you wish to pay but you cannot guarantee that any trades will be made and the order is filled. That may be preferable to having a filled order completed at a higher price than you wanted, but sometimes a partially filled order may be a worse outcome.

A limit order can, however, be quite flexible in so much as it can be made into an all-or-none (AON) type of order. This changes the fundamental behavior of a basic limit order because what the AON attribute means is that unless the order can get all the 100 Facebook shares at the price you specified, in this case, $140, then you won't agree to buy any of the shares. For example, in the previous example, if we had made our limit order AON for the Facebook stock, it would not buy the 50 shares that were offered until the full order could have been completed, i.e., when and another 50 shares become available at the fixed price you are bidding.

Now that may seem straightforward, but this is where the complexity of trading comes into play. Remember you are trading on a market where you are buying or selling shares to other traders. The problem is if the price of the stock you are holding starts to fall and you try to sell on a limit order with a fixed price offer to sell at $139 then you might find it difficult to find a buyer and you would have missed the opportunity to exit the trade and minimize your losses. However, had you used a market offer you would have found a buyer at the best price available though that may be at the lower price of $138.50. On the other hand; if you were confident that a stock would rise in value, and you used a limit order at $140 to bid, you may well find that there are no offers at that price, as the market is turning and the current lowest price is now $140.50 so you will again have missed out on the opportunity to claim the stock. Should the stock continue to rise and the next day it goes up to $145 you will have missed out on significant profit, which would not have been the case had you used a market offer.

Limit orders are therefore primarily used by traders who are more concerned with the price they want to pay for or sell stock rather than the number of shares they want. Price versus getting the order filled is the primary trade-offs between market and limit orders.

Stop Orders

Stock trading carries risk as price movements can be volatile and as swing traders, we do not want to be tied to a screen every minute of the working day. To reduce and manage risk, we can use a mechanism called Stop Orders. These are orders that are executed only when the stock price movement meets a certain price level. Upon reaching this price criterion - the stop price - this will automatically trigger the trade. Hence the behavior of a stop order is that it will remain dormant until the stock price has reached the pre-set stop price. At this point, it essentially turns into a market order, which is then automatically filled at the best available price so that you can bale out of the position as safely as possible. For example, should you decide to protect some shares that are currently worth $18 and you place a stop-loss order at $16, your tactics are to automatically trigger a market order once the stock drops below $16, which hopefully would ensure that losses did not exceed much beyond the $2 per share.

This mechanism or order type is also known as a stop-loss order, for as we have just demonstrated this allows you to limit your losses.

Moreover, this type of order can not only limit losses it can also be used to safeguard profits. For example, if you have bought a stock at $15 but the stock is currently trading at $25. If you now make a stop order at $22 this will lock-in actual profits of around $7 per share. However this is also dependent on their being buyers at that price, if not it will fill the order at the best available price, but in theory, the practice is sound. As a result, the usage of stop orders is of particular interest and advantage to investors who are unable to take a hands-on approach to manage their stocks.

However, as we have seen, a stop order transforms into a market order so it will be filled at the best available price. This means that the price received may well be lower than the price that you intended to get when you activated the stop order. Moreover, traders must give setting the stop order level considerable thought as it can prove counterproductive if set incorrectly. For example, if the stock is known to be volatile and historically fluctuates long term around 15%, and you were to set the stop-loss at a level of 10% below the current price then the order is likely to be activated unintentionally or at least prematurely by a sudden short term dip in price. This might not sound too bad but if you had patiently nurtured a position just waiting for an upturn in the market then unintentionally exited the trade due to a poorly positioned stop-order just before that big surge in the price you were expecting then you will have missed out on profit, which may be particularly infuriating.

Other Kinds of Orders

There are several other types of orders that the beginner swing trader should become familiar. For example, orders can have other attributes applied to them to adjust their behavior. One common attribute is regarding how long an order will remain valid. This can operate like a kill switch as in an immediate-or-cancel (IOC) order. In this case, the order's attribute makes sure the order is canceled if it isn't fulfilled right away. When an IOC order is used in combination with an AON order, it will become a 'fill-or-kill' (FOK) order. A classic example of such an order is used in day trading where each day's orders have a limit or stop order that cancels the order at the end of the day to ensure no orders can survive till the next day. A good-till-canceled (GTC) order, on the other hand, will remain active until it is instructed to cancel.

Margin Trading and Short Selling

In all types of trading, you will need to set up a trading account with a broker. Regulations in some countries will insist on a specific minimum amount. The amount you have in the account will limit the trades that you can make as the sum of the stock prices as well as the corresponding commissions and/or transaction fees cannot exceed the balance in your trading account.

Many brokerages, however, offer a service called margin trading, which allows their traders to use their accounts as collateral so that they can borrow money to trade shares. Margin trading is typically set at around 4:1 which allows positions to be bought using 4 times the amount of cash in the client's account. For day traders' using margin, trading is considered to be high risk, but many do it anyway as it greatly enhances their trading power. High risk often equates to high losses and in margin trading high debt.

Nonetheless, margin accounts can be utilized in other ways as they also enable a technique called short selling, which is where you can borrow shares to sell them. The trick here is that you will be gambling on the price of the stock continues to fall. If the conditions are right, you will be able to sell the borrowed shares then buy the shares back in the future at an even lower price. A short seller is, in essence, betting that the downtrend will continue and the price will continue to fall so they will make a profit on the difference between the prices when they return the borrowed stock.

Bulls and Bears

As a beginner trader, you will hear many new terms, and none is perhaps more intriguing and less intuitive that the term of Bulls and Bears. These labels are used to describe from a very general perspective the relative current status of the market. This is often required because even expert investors often disagree about the value of particular stocks, segments or even about the direction of the economy in general.

As a result, each trading day is a battle between optimists and pessimists, and when the former dominates the trading, then the result is that prices trend upwards, and then we say that we are in a bull market. When the opposite is true, and the pessimist's gain the upper hand then prices will trend downwards, and then we are said to be in a bear market.

A bull market results when time and the economic indicators are good such as when unemployment is low, domestic product (GDP) is growing, and subsequently, the price of stocks are rising. Under these conditions picking stocks is arguably easier because everything is going up. During a bull market the optimist believes that stocks will continue to go up, so they can be said to have a bullish outlook. But rising bull markets cannot last forever, and if stocks become overvalued, they can lead to dangerous dips in stock value and worse loss of trading confidence.

One severe and dangerous form of a bull market is known as a bubble. This is where the upward trend of the stock prices and the subsequent optimism no longer conforms to rational trading fundamentals. Examples of bubbles are the dot.com boom in 2000, the mortgage overvaluations in 2008 and the Bitcoin mania in late 2017. Consequently, due to their irrationally high over-valuation, these bubbles will always burst when reality finally catches up with their overinflated prices.

From the other perspective, we can say that we have a bear market when there is a 20% drop in broad market indices such as the SP500. Typically a bear market is realized due to poor national economic results such as when unemployment rises, corporate profits are falling, and the GDP growth is stunted, and this is normally an omen that the economy appears to be in or very near recession.

From your swing trading perspective, however, a bear market means it will be very risky to pick profitable stocks. The way the professionals get around this problem and still profit from when stocks are falling is via short selling, which we discussed earlier. However, that is a dodgy business for the beginner. Another more likely strategy is to wait until you feel that the bear market is nearing its end, only starting to buy in anticipation of a return to a bull market. The problem being however is in identifying a bull from a bear market in the first place.

The huge problem for beginner traders when contemplating bear markets is that the condition naturally increases stock market volatility. But prices do not drop in an orderly or rational way but rather collapse as a result of market traders overreacting in a panic that sends prices crashing. Unfortunately, this type of irrational behavior is contagious, and whole market sectors may inevitably collapse. It will only be when rational investing behavior that relates to fundamentals is restored that a bear market does a turnaround. However, those low prices during a bear market are great opportunities for long-term investors to buy stocks, for they will eventually become good and this can boost overall returns if you're willing to play the longer game of position trading.

Summary

In this chapter, we have introduced you to the mechanics behind financial trading and how it works. We have also shown how you can manipulate your trades to your advantage as well as introduce you to the elementary features of risk management through the use of different types of orders. None of this probably makes much sense at the moment, but later on, you will appreciate this early grounding in the basics.

Chapter 2 - What is Swing Trading?

In the previous chapter, we introduced you to the rudimentary mechanics of how financial trading works. In this chapter, we will take a step forward and introduce you to the techniques of swing trading. In doing so, we will show you the pros and cons of being a swing trader against the other types of trading styles. However, to best demonstrate the techniques of swing trading we will focus on trading in high-value stocks as they are less volatile, but the methods and strategies are the same as if you were trading on currencies or any other financial instrument. So understand that the swing trading methods and strategies we recommend can be applied to trading in any financial market.

Introduction to Swing Trading

Now that we have been introduced to the basic theory behind how the financial markets work and understand the difference between bullish and bearish forces, we can now move on to take a look at how swing trading works.

The concept behind swing trading is based upon the fluctuations or waves found in an upward or downward trend. These waves are caused by price fluctuations that can be found in any financial market, but for the sake of brevity, we will only concern ourselves with the stock markets. However, the principles apply to any form of swing trading in financial instruments.

Stock prices caused by bullish or bearish forces are driven in their respective directions by variations in demand. Unfortunately, these waves of demand are not symmetrical and easy to determine let alone predict, but they still exist. What's more is that once the wave is identified, it tends to repeat itself. For example, in an upward trend, there will be brief periods where the stock price's upwards path falters briefly and even drops. These brief interruptions are called pull-backs. It is during one of these pull-backs that the stock price dips before rallying once more. This can be seen if you study the stock's price-line over time. The upward trend, in this case, would not be a nice symmetrical wave but more like a jagged sawtooth with many pull-backs – those are representative of the battles between bulls and bears - along with the general upward trend line.

Therefore we can consider any uptrend to be a series of pull-backs where each successive rally sends the stock price higher than the previous one hence the upward trend. Importantly each pull-back will also stop higher than the previous pull-back. So, in an upward trend, we can consider that each successive pull-back will have higher-high prices and higher-low prices than its predecessor as we progress along the timeline.

In swing trading, the goal is to identify and then capitalize on the predictability of that pattern. To do this, you will need to buy stock during the pull-back when the price is dropping and ideally at the lowest point of the pull-back. You then hold the stock until the next highest point and sell just before the next pull-back to maximize your profits.

However, you can also trade during a downward (bear) trend as they also exhibit the same predictable wave characteristics. The basic difference is that the downward trend is interrupted by many brief up-lifts where the stock price rallies before dropping once more. In this case, a downtrend can be identified by a series of lower lows and lower highs at the peak of each pull-up. When we swing a trade during a downtrend, the idea is to sell short during a pull-up. We will discuss the mechanics of selling short in detail later.

But before we get ahead of ourselves let's put what we have learned together and see what we require to start out in swing trading.

Identifying the trends

First, we will need to identify a stock that is ideal to trade and displays all the characteristics of an uptrend or a downtrend. For example with stocks in an uptrend, we will want to identify those that are experiencing a pull-back or for stocks in a downtrend we want to look for those that are experiencing a pull-up. However, this is easier said than done as all of the current methods used to identify stocks appropriate for swing trading are based on reading charts using a technique called technical analysis.

Technical analysis is a method that uses analysis tools working on the historical price/volume data to identify the hidden patterns of up-pull/down-pull behavior. Isolating these behavioral patterns enables us to predict the trend and consequently the future behavior. This might sound very complicated, but there are many tools available to do the heavy-lifting of technical analysis for you. Thankfully it is not necessary for you to be a technical analysis guru to swing trade. We will cover these tools later in the book once we have got the essential theory out of the way.

The Right Stocks for Swing Trading

Swing trading methods are about making stock positions which will be held for longer than a single day and up to perhaps a few weeks at most. Therefore the most essential ingredient for successful swing trading is choosing the right stocks to trade. The best stocks to trade in are typically large-cap stocks, which are the shares of a company with a market capitalization in excess of $5 billion. The capitalization figure is determined by multiplying the company's stock price against the number of shares. Large-cap stocks are among the most actively traded stocks on the major exchanges. Because of their high trading rates, they trade well in an active market.

This makes these stocks attractive for beginners and the less experienced because even the big money players cannot unduly affect the market direction. This is simply because the large institutions cannot buy or sell their large volumes quickly enough to create volatility. As a result, large-cap stocks will swing creating the potential profits we want but only within the safe narrow spread between high and low prices.

As swing traders, we will want to trade with the trend in one direction for a couple of days or weeks. Then we might reevaluate and switch to the opposite flow when we see that the major trend of the trade reverses direction. It is advisable for beginners to always go with the flow of direction and not to try to buck the major trends.

Choosing the Right Market

We were introduced to the concept of the bull and bear markets earlier. In either of the two market condition, even the most active stocks will not experience the same up-pulls and down-pulls – the opportunities for profit - as the major trend flow is upwards or downwards. In either case, this trend will persist for a long period in one direction only. This is why it is important not to buck the trend and that the best strategy is to trade on the existent longer-term trend.

However, there are periods when the market trends are going nowhere. In this case, it is neither bullish nor bearish, and this is when conditions may also be optimal for the swing trader. This is because stock price indexes will rise for a few days and then there is a short period of decline over the next few days. These frequent up-pulls and down-pulls in the trend repeat the same general pattern over time. Despite there being no overall gain in the stock price the swing trader has had many opportunities to catch the short-term price movements during the more frequent up and down activity. Of course, the problem is correctly identifying what type of market is currently being experienced.

Swing trading is still one of the most effective trading styles for the beginning trader. Nonetheless, it still offers significant opportunities for profit to more experienced traders. And this is essentially what swing trading is all about.

Why Swing Trade and not Day Trade

Before you decide to swing trade, it is important to understand the difference between swing and day trading and pick the best fit for you. The main difference is in the timeline as swing traders will work on stock price movements over periods greater than one day. The day-trader will work on stock variations during the market opening times for example from 9.00 to 16-00 and always close out at their positions at the end of every day.

However, because the day trader is working on such tight timelines, the focus required is very demanding. As a result, a day trader will typically be watching several screens all day long prepared to react to any sudden price volatility. This is because day traders are working to tight timescales that requires changing their positions often. Perhaps they are working on one, three or five-minute intervals to ensure their stocks stay in a profitable position. This means that too successfully day trade requires commitment and focus, and so it is almost a full-time job.

On the other hand, a swing trader is concerned with changes to their position over several days. This means they can take a much more relaxed and hands-off approach to monitor stock price movements. Of course, they must still monitor their stock position to ensure it remains in a profitable position, but there are much more leeway and breathing space. This is very important as it means critical stock position decisions can be more informed and less stressful than with day trading.

Remember that the day traders are competing against the large market players and the big boys like hedge funds and high-frequency traders. These guys are serious professionals more likely today they are algorithms, and if you're an individual seriously wishing to compete with these financial institutions with all their trading advantages, you're going to have to spend a lot of money to get the technology. Swing traders, on the other hand, can easily get by on just traditional home computer hardware and technology along with a subscription service for trading advice and a broker account.

Commitment and startup costs are not the only benefits of swing trading, however, as another very important one is the risk. We will cover risk and risk management in detail later in the book, but for now, we will highlight the inherent dangers of any type of trading.

In day trading stock can move rapidly and that means inexperienced or uncommitted day traders can lose money just as fast. This is one reason that many financial regulators now require a day trader to have a minimum of $25,000 on account with their brokerage. This is far higher than the $2,000 requirement for swing traders as it reflects the significant difference in risk. Worse, of course, is that day traders tend to resort to trading on margins – borrowed money in effect. The way this works is that the brokerages will typically offer the day trader a 4:1 margin. So in effect, they can finance trades up to 4 x their $25,000 account and although this can be a great benefit – provides the money to buy into bigger positions that leads to greatly increased profits. Hence, working on the margin can be highly beneficial for experienced day traders, but it can be disastrous for rookie traders as it also greatly magnifies losses.

Also, there are other benefits to swing trading; one significant benefit is that you as a swing trader will receive sufficient feedback on your trades over a couple of days to keep you focused and motivated. On the other hand, day trading where you will be trading dozens of stocks per day may prove too overwhelming and too stressful for most beginners.

Swing Trading Vs. Position or Trend Trading

There is, of course, another style of trading that takes a much longer perspective on how long to hold a position. This is called position or trend trading as it is the one favored by hedge funds and large financial institutions. However, there is nothing to stop you from adopting a position style of trading.

The idea behind position trading is that the trader is entering the position for the long run. Typically, they will be buying a large amount of stock in the company as they seek longer-term profits.

This might be because they think the company is undervalued because it is underperforming due to market conditions or through a lack of financial investment or perhaps, they are just enthused by the company's product or business plan.

A good example of a position trader is Warren Buffett as he invests long term using his billions of dollars. However, moving that amount of investment is problematic as it would hugely distort the market value of any single company. As a result, institutions will often position trade by buying small batches of stock on a regular basis. This has the effect of keeping the target company's stock stable but does introduce all those little interruptions that are the bread and butter opportunities for the swing trader.

Retail vs. Institutional Traders

Now that we know the styles of trading that goes on in the financial markets we can take some time to consider the different types of trader. These are the people performing the trading, and there are two types that you will see being referred to in the media. Firstly there are the institutional traders. This category includes Wall Street banks, mutual funds, proprietary trading firms, as well as hedge funds. It is by far the biggest group of traders. This type of trader has many advantages one of which is that they have all the resources behind them to create advanced trading algorithms to help them execute transactions in the blink of an eye. However, institutional traders are not just those working for these large financial institutions but also include professionals working with another people's capital.

The second much smaller group is what is called Retail Traders, and these people are independent traders using their own money and work for themselves. They may well be professional and full time, but many are part-time amateurs (hobbyists). What they do all have in common is that in addition to their independence they have none of the vast financial or technological advantages of the institutional trader.

However retail traders do have an advantage in trading style in so much as they are free to select their own targets – capital permitting. An example of this constraint for the institutional traders is that many institutions are only interested in large investments and will have no interest in taking a position of 1,000 shares in a company trading less than 500k shares a day, it is just too small. However, the retail trader can seize that opportunity as they have no such constraints. On the contrary, the retail trader can take any position they feel that gives them a good risk to reward ration and thus an opportunity for profit.

Furthermore, some institutions such as mutual funds may not be allowed to buy into firms with capital valuation under a set amount, and this leaves gaps in the market and opportunity for the retail traders to exploit. Unfortunately, many retail traders fail to leverage these advantages and succumb to trading unwisely. In this way, they often end up going head to head with the mighty institutional traders instead of patiently picking the low hanging fruits. By failing to select appropriate targets the retail trader almost inevitable overtrades through lack of self-discipline. To be successful in the financial markets, the retail traders must be patient and understand the philosophies of greed and fear and how they drive the markets.

Summary

At this point you should now know what swing trading is about and if it fits with your personality and risk appetite. If for example, you thrive on the excitement of making gut-feeling decisions then day trading may be for you. At the other extreme, you may prefer to exhaustively research a company and analyze the annual figures before you commit to a trade, in which case a positional trader may be a better option. Neither is right or wrong it depends on your personal risk appetite, but swing trading can be seen as a compromise. Using swing trading, you can have the short term elation of a good win and also the satisfaction of making a well-researched trade.

Chapter 3 - Finding a suitable Market

In the previous chapter, we discussed swing trading techniques and how they differ from other trading styles. However financial markets have very different behaviors, and some are more appropriate to swing trading than others. Therefore in this chapter, we will look at some appropriate markets in which you can as a beginner start swing trading. No bias favors a particular market; we will leave that up to you. Instead, we will try to evaluate what are and are not feasible markets for you to enter based on your initial capital.

Selecting a Financial Instrument to trade

Selecting a market in which to trade will be the first big decision you will have to make as there are several different financial markets and what they call financial instruments to choose to trade in. For instance, you can trade in shares, currency, futures, options or even crypto-currencies to name just a few. Which one you choose will depend on your interest in that field and also largely by the capital you have to trade.

The good news is that there are lots of financial instruments you can swing trade with. And each one of them has its own pros and cons. Here are some financial instruments that are considered suitable for swing trading:

Exchange-Traded Funds (ETFs): You can trade ETFs just as you would trade a regular company's stock such as Facebook (FB) or Apple Inc. (AAPL). There are ETFs for just about everything; they will track indexes and bonds, futures, commodities, stock sectors, and currencies.

Individual stocks: Possibly the most popular instrument for swing trading is trading individual company shares. There are some advantages and disadvantages to trading individual stocks compared to trading ETFs. For example, taking a position with an individual stock exposes you to the possibility of 'single event risk.' What this means is that if you are holding a long position on a trending stock, you can be vulnerable to sudden bad news. For example, if bad news about a security breach breaks, say regarding Facebook or Google, the stock can suddenly fall. However, if you were swing trading on a sector like technology that bad news might take time to affect the market. The point is that when trading individual stocks, you are always going to be vulnerable to this type of single event risk. On the other hand, typically individual stocks can outperform other companies stocks that are in the same sector such as Technology. This means that taking a position on an individual company's stock may mean that you can outperform an ETF covering the related sector.

Currencies: Forex trading is another hugely popular swing trading instrument. When trading Forex, you are comparing the relative performances of two currencies, and so you are looking for one currency to move up or down relative to the other currency. But this requires a huge amount of research into international financial markets, and it is very volatile. For example, the US dollar may go sky high or plummet compared to the Euro on the basis of a late-night tweet by a President or a CEO. Forex trading is high risk and volatile, but that also makes it attractive and if you are on the right side of the trade extremely profitable.

Cryptocurrencies: Swing trading these new cryptocurrencies has opened up a whole new market which has attracted very professional, sophisticated but also some very dubious traders and investors. The huge attraction of vast and quick profit has many amateurs entering the market which hugely inflated the realistic price. Nonetheless, the volatility of cryptocurrencies is a dream for swing traders so long as you don't get greedy.

Some of the more popular coins include, but there are many more:
- Bitcoin
- Ethereum
- Bitcoin Cash
- Ripple

Bitcoin, in particular, hit a bubble around the end of 2017 which resulted in about 80% of its value being wiped out during the 2018 backlash. Consequently, the steep price reversal led to a loss of confidence in trading cryptocurrencies, so interest has dropped significantly. But Bitcoin, in particular, has always been of interest to swing traders due to its regular periods of high price volatility for seemingly no discernible reason. Where may that put many a beginner? There are also plenty seeking potentially huge profits. As a result, Bitcoin and the other cryptocurrencies still have the potential for high price movements for swing trading.

Options: Options and Futures are a more sophisticated instrument that can be used in hedge funds and hedging positions, but they are also good for swing trading. Trading options and using them in a variety of strategies requires additional education and experience that are not quite covered here, but as a swing trader you should be aware of their existence and consider using them as you increase your knowledge.

How much Capital will I need?

This is one of the most common questions beginners ask, but there is no real satisfactory answer as it depends. The reason it depends is that the market or financial instrument you decide to trade in will largely decide what is and isn't a viable starting capital account. For example, if we take a beginner with only $1,000 of capital which must be considered as being disposable income – only trade with what you are prepared to lose – then the only viable financial instrument to trade safely is currencies using the Forex market. We say 'safely' because to avoid the risk of ruin you must only risk 1% of your capital per trade – we will explain this in detail later. Therefore, you can only in this case risk $10 per trade. Now that might not sound too bad, but we have to take the commissions and transaction costs into play. We can demonstrate this through a few examples:

If you have $1000 in your broker account, this means that you should limit yourself to $10 or 1% on each trade. But given a $1000 account size, it reduces your option to trade different financial instruments for example:

Shares

Minimum size: 100 shares

Transaction cost: $50 per round trip (buy/sell)

The transaction costs are far larger than you're allowed risk per trade. Remember you can only risk $10 per trade.

Also, the transaction costs will take a huge amount of your profits. So if you're making around 50 trades per week, you will need a return of between 150%-200% to break even.

Futures

Minimum size: 1 lot

Transaction cost: $10 per round trip

With Futures, your transaction costs eat up 1% of your return before you even start trading. And if you're making 50 trades per week, you will need a return of 50% to break even.

Forex

Minimum size: 1000 units

Transaction cost: Average 3 pips is around 30 cents

The transactions costs make trading deals on the Forex feasible as the transaction costs are small relative to your allowed risk ($10).

Therefore it might be feasible to trade Forex with a $1000 account.

But here is the problem; Forex is a volatile market and a beginner with a capital fund of $1,000 is likely to be wiped out in a matter of weeks.

There is a simple mathematical formula that can be useful when evaluating feasible instruments so that you can trade safely:

1. First, work out your risk appetite by deciding how much you are willing to lose and set the stop-loss order at an appropriate level – but keep in mind that you might not get that price as you are trying to sell when the market is not keen to buy.

2. Secondly, factor in your broker's transaction costs; this is applied to every trade
3. Add the two figures together, and if the sum is less than 1% of your current trading account, then you can consider the instrument to be feasible to trade safely.

However, what is a feasible minimum capital account and what is recommended are two completely different things. For example, a capital fund of $2,000 is feasible for swing trading in shares, if the transaction rates are lower than some online broker's platform that operates with a minimum account of $1,000 and charges as little as $3.75 per transaction. However, entering the market with such small capital will restrict the number of trades that are available to you as ideally, you would want to trade the large Cap stock which is less vulnerable to market price manipulation by the market makers. Consequently, many experts recommend a starting capital account as an absolute minimum of $8,000 for trading shares.

Tools and Platforms you will need

If you are seriously entering the market, then you should do it professionally. You should consider it the way you would any other business start-up venture. Therefore you must have the capital, knowledge and the tools to do the job. The first thing you will need is an account with a licensed broker as they will do the trades on your behalf. They will also provide you with a way to make the trades typically through an online system. You should, however, shop about and try their online simulators to make sure you are comfortable with the system and the information that they give you. Fortunately, online brokers and stock trading platforms are in abundance, but your choice may be restricted by the country in which you are currently residing.

However, if you are just starting out and you do not have a trading account, then do a Google search to find a broker in your country that has good reviews.

When considering a broker look for the following things:
Account type – There are several types of accounts that are available to you as a swing trader. There will be an investment account. This style of account allows you to trade within the limits of cash deposited in the account. However, there is also an account called a Margin Account which allows you to use the money or stocks in your account as collateral so that you can borrow money from the broker. This facility of getting a loan from the broker will give you more trading power; however, you must be aware that you are now trading on borrowed money. This means you are taking on far more risk.

Transaction fees – The cost of executing a trade must be taken into account as the commission can vary greatly in price between brokers. However, for a swing trader that is just starting out the transaction fees are not quite so important. This is simply because as a beginner you should only be doing a very limited amount of small transactions a month. If not and you start out over trading then the brokers' transactions fee are likely to eat up the majority of your profit. The good news is that there are online brokers that charge as little as $3.75 per trade, but the bad news is that if you are working off a $1,000 account and sticking to the safe 1% rule, even that small commission will take most if not all of your profit.

Platforms and Tools – You want a trading system that you are comfortable with, but they vary a lot. Some online trading systems give you a lot of added features such as charts and research. Others, however, will give you the bare minimum. Also, the quality of advice and tools can vary across different brokerages. Indeed it is not just across brokerages as some firms will offer different classes of service depending on how much you're willing to pay. Nonetheless, to start out you will want a reliable online system that provides real-time quotes as well as a straight forward ordering procedure. It is also important to have a reliable system that will execute your orders immediately and also confirm your trades. That is the minimum you should be looking for, but it would be nice to have real-time charts, technical analysis tools (moving averages, support/resistance, etc.). If you are going to pay a lot for the broker's services, then you should expect research reports and opinions as well as their analysts' ratings. Fortunately finding a broker and online services is not difficult as there are many free resources and online tools available. Listed below are several excellent resources.

Finviz (finviz.com)
ChartMill (chartmill.com)
StockCharts.com (stockcharts.com)
Estimize (estimize.com)
StockTwits (stocktwits.com)
CNBC (CNBC.com)
Yahoo Finance (finance.yahoo.com)

Practice, practice, and then practice some more

Before you use your account, you need to use the broker's online simulator or start out paper trading to learn and find your risk tolerance and develop your early skills.

Traditionally the way beginners' entered the market was via an apprenticeship and spent paper trading, but today demo accounts are preferred. Nonetheless, paper trading is still an excellent way to find out if swing trading is suitable for you as it does provide valuable feedback on your trading judgment before you put your real money at risk. However, paper trading goes against the grain with many beginners to swing trading as it lacks the excitement of the real thing. Nonetheless, if you are serious about making swing trading a profitable venture then delay opening a trading account until you have practiced and believe that you are ready to start live trading.

Starting out Paper Trading

Practicing and learning the art or science behind swing trading is incredibly important. After all, what makes you think as a novice that you can just enter the market and beat the odds. The harsh reality is that you will need to practice and then learn from your mistakes. It is those defeats and your subsequent analysis that will give you the skills which will enable you to survive let alone be successful. Even if you are a skilled trader in other instruments or a hugely successful day or position trader changing codes means learning new strategies and specialized tactics. Nonetheless, as competitive as the markets are, paper trading does give you a method to practice and develop your skills. This is why and how you should do it:

- Before you, as a beginner place a live trade, you should make sure to take the time to test the waters by first trying trading out on paper. The first step is to decide the amount you want to trade. This amount will be determined ultimately by your capital and your risk appetite. But in this
- example let us keep the figures easy to work with so let's say it is $10,000
- Then you go about selecting your stock after some level of fundamental analysis you have concluded that certain stocks look to be on a promising trend wave and worth trading.
- Now what you have to do is to write on paper or notepad the current stock prices and the number of shares you want to buy with their current selling price.
- Then you must subtract the commission and transaction fees from that figure.
- Divide that trading figure by the actual share price, but remember to round down as you can't own a 1/3 or 1/2 of a share.
- Then sit back and ride the wave as you track your trades. You can easily do this by checking the closing stock price.

An example of Paper Trading To let you see how well it can work here is an example of paper trading a virtual portfolio.

In this scenario, you will start with say $20,000 and five preferred stocks. You have $4,000 per investment, but we must take commission and transaction fees into the equation, so we are less a $20 fee for buying and selling that's $9,980 apiece. Hence, we are likely to buy along with this type of pattern:

Stock A: Bought 100 shares at $20 for $2000
Stock B: Bought 150 shares at $30 for $4500
Stock C: Bought 100 shares at $50 for $5000
Stock D: Bought 100 shares at $60 for $6000
Stock E: Bought 200 shares at $12 for $2400

Now what you want to keep in mind here is that the original share price isn't as significant as the percentage of price movement, i.e., the gain or loss. For example, if Stock B goes up from $4 to $34 per share. You now have $5100 in this position a profit of 11%. But the notable thing is if Stock E also goes up from $4 to $16 per share? Well, then you'd be at $3,200 in this position at a profit of 13%.

This is the thing you must remember it isn't always just about the price it is about your current position – this is determined by both the price and how much stock you hold. Paper trading is educational and can be helpful in surfacing some strange trading anomalies as well as effectively designing your own swing-trading strategy. After all, it is far better to make your mistakes on paper exercises than lose your money trading real stocks. Of course, there is a downside. It is boring, and you don't get the positive feedback that a real trade gives you – a tangible loss or gain – but you must practice and learn the skills and develop those tactics and then see whether your skills and research return a profit. An alternative approach and one many younger people favor is to use a simulator or demo account to test your skills.

Practice trading with a Demo Account

Should you find that paper trading is a bit boring, then an alternative is to use a demo account. Most brokers will give you this facility as it is a simulator that you can practice on. By all accounts, demo accounts are more enticing than paper trading as the simulators give you immediate feedback as to how your trades are performing. But of course, there is always a conflict of interest – remember they are trying to sell you a service - and you may well find that you can do no wrong. Instead, you should try out as many as you can, and practice swing trading with a wide range of tactics. At the end of the day, demo accounts are a great way to gain trading experience without losing your money. They are important to swing traders as they allow you to try out and experiment with new strategies and tactics. They also help you build confidence –

but be aware some are vanity orientated - while you learn the basics of market trading.

Demos - are they realistic?

The problem with simulators and demo market games is that they are often too one dimensional. They do not sufficiently give the experience of actually losing or winning and one of the problems is they often have little context as the data is historical. But in real life, the market is based on three emotions; Greed, Fear and Hope. With the latter being the deadliest. There is no way to simulate these emotions at the depth required to represent real trading whereby you could be fabulously wealthy or wiped out in a few seconds. Instead, the best that demo accounts can do is to simulate the real trading environment without the emotions. It is not the same psychologically. Indeed physically trading with pretend money in many ways can make you learn bad habits. Nonetheless, it is an introduction to the sometimes-overwhelming experience of the financial market's mayhem. Therefore, realistic or not it is still a very good way to practice. There is, of course, a dilemma as most brokers provide you with these free to use demos or simulators. The problem is that they want you to play and to boost your confidence and get you to trade. After all, that's how they make their money.

Hence be very wary of demos where you seem to do no wrong and especially those that reward a winning trade with a pop up acclaiming you to be a top trader.

Discovery – There is a school of thought that every trader should find their niche market by testing their skills and knowledge against different financial instruments. The belief is that it will allow you to get a feel for the market that is best suited to your temperament as markets do behave differently. An example would be that trading stocks will be different to futures or commodities.

Gain experience – Practice your techniques and strategies on paper or a demo before you risk your own money. Whatever you do practice at least entering and exiting positions, plus applying stops and limits. Also, you may want to start experimenting with short selling, but most importantly you will gain an understanding of risk and capital margin requirements, as well as in tracking your profit and loss.

Charting – The most important aspect that a beginner to trading needs to learn is how to read a chart. Even if it is just simple pattern recognition, it is invaluable in making informed decisions. Therefore you should spend time learning how to interpret price charts. What is more, you should also test your tactics and techniques against these charts to validate their effectiveness by testing the technical indicators to surface illusive patterns.

Evaluate past performance – Just about all worthy analysis is based on historical data. Machine Learning and A.I. feed almost exclusively on historical data. These clever algorithms analyze past performance data to find ways to find better solutions. They also are a good way to determine and then hone your strategy before you put your savings on the line.

Trading tools – There are a myriad of resources available to you such as the financial news, forums, and social media but how you interpret the information is the decisive factor. We all have free access to the same general information, but some make it work for
them while others let it drift by. Understanding how world events can affect stocks particularly within a sector is hugely important, so pay attention to news feeds and breaking market data.

Watch-lists – As part of your overall strategy have a list of potential stock that you would like to keep an eye on. These may be stocks that you aren't sure about, but you still should keep them in mind. Many experienced traders regrets are over missed opportunities rather than bad trades so keep track of those borderline stocks.

Manage Risk – A demo account is hugely beneficial as you are betting with virtual money. Therefore gains and losses are meaningless in real terms, but they should be tactically analyzed to prevent you from repeating the mistake with your own money. Also, demos allow you to practice swing trading so that you make your early learning mistakes in a safe environment and not in the big bad world.

Price action – Demos can give you plenty of practice in reading price lines and identifying trends. One of the best ways to interpret a price line is to spot the visual patterns; however, that only comes with experience. Practicing on real price lines on a demo will give you plenty of practice interpreting those volatile movements that will allow you to profit on future real price fluctuations.

Broker and platform – Trying out a broker's online platform is a good way to evaluate their service. You can, for example, see what research and charts they provide and also see what they charge extra for. Also you can get a taste of how good they are by dipping into their forum and taking account of the sentiments of the regular poster.

Strategy

Test before you play – This is a great advantage that you as a swing trader have in your favor as it means you have time on your side. So leverage that and test before you commit to a trade. You might hear on a forum of some miracle indicator or fool-proof method to beat the market but always try it out on the demo first. Demos are a perfect place for experimentation as losses cost you nothing. Hence they are perfect for trying out new tactics or adjusting your strategy. Always test before you trade as even the best looking metrics can turn out to be rubbish when used out of context. Remember some of the greatest and successful swing traders use a combination of ten or even twenty metrics when evaluating a trade. But even they admit it can be confusing so always test a new tactic before you trade. Using a demo account will enable you to try out new things without risking losing your money. After all most trading mistakes come about due to over exuberance which leads to overtrading or through fear where profits are cut short. Another flaw is in a beginner steadfastly adhering to a directional bias, which can also be detrimental if you haven't practiced – and learned about trends and reversals -on a demo accounts beforehand.

Backward/Forward testing – Another great use for a demo account is for backward or forwards testing. The idea here is that once you have a tactic or change in strategy in mind, you can either backtest against historical data or forward test your trading plan using forecasting. While backtesting is very useful as you are working on objective data, it does tend to lack emotional excitement. On the other hand, forward testing is about projections, and this enables you to put your battle-plan into action in real-time. As a beginner however you should always stick to backward testing till you gain experience.

Drawdowns – There will be days where the market is working against you or psychologically you are just not up for the fight. However, these are the days when experimenting with new tactics on the demo account can pay dividends. You might discover a new metric that turns your trading average around or more likely see how you would be better adjusting your position size until things turn around.

Drawbacks to Demo Accounts

Now we have just spent the last few paragraphs telling you how great demo simulations are, but unfortunately, there are some downsides. Therefore before you go rushing out to get hold of a demo account on which to learn swing trading, you need to read this. Demo accounts for swing trading do have certain important limitations:

Execution – Demo accounts do not always relate to real-world conditions. This is because demo accounts are virtual, so they relate to the data at hand, so they usually fill a market order at a price offered. However, in the real world there is not always a buyer conveniently there to meet your asking price so, in a live market, there is some amount of slippage. This slippage means that some orders are not being filled immediately at the price that you wanted. Of course with falling stock, this means there are more sellers than buyers, which will make matching a deal more difficult. This makes setting loss-orders that meet actual levels of risk very challenging.

Unlimited capital – One of the strange things about online demos is that they provide you by default with vast capital to play with. Now there is a good reason for this. The reason they give you almost unlimited virtual funds is that gains are accelerated and losses can be easily recuperated if you have sufficient funds. This is what is called the risk to ruin ratio; should you bet $10 and lose the bet you will need on your next bet to cover that loss as well as get the expected gain and with limited funds this soon becomes unfeasible.

Dubious Data –Many brokers host dubious demos where you basically can do no wrong. These types of vanity sites are deliberately enticing you to trade with them based on a false premise – that you are good.

Deposits – Although you should always be practicing using virtual money some brokers will require an initial deposit or your credit card details to use their demo accounts. If that is the case, then you should walk away.

Leverage – Many beginners get caught up in the initial winning streak on demos and seem to enjoy the irrational behavior of the system as they enjoy ever-increasing success. While this can instill confidence and result in substantial virtual profits, it does not transport well to a live-trading environment where it will almost certainly lead to significant losses.

Unfulfilled Orders – In demo accounts, everything is a virtual reality so if you trade at a price the order will be fulfilled. But in the real world things are more complex, and often there are no buyers for the stock you want to sell - at least at that price. Therefore trades in a demo always go through as executed. However, when live trading, orders will often go unfulfilled.

Trading tools – All those charts and research that you got in your demo account will suddenly come at an additional cost when you switch to live trading.

Market movements – Demo simulators are just that; simulations of the market so they do not always have real-time data, so your demo account server may not take into account up to the minute changes. These can include updates on out of hour's price movements.

Psychological effects

Emotions –The three emotions behind trading are Fear, Hope, and Greed that you may experience when you live trade. The fear of losing your capital is understandable so only trade what you can afford to lose. Greed, on the other hand, can make you ride a wave for too long. But it is hoped that is the deadliest of all. Demo accounts cannot replicate this toxic environment.

Risk Management – Complacency is another major sin, if you do not take your trades seriously, you may overlook potential unclaimed profits or overlook potential trends. However with a practice account and diligent practice these flaws can be overcome. It is a simple fact that beginner traders will be more risk tolerant trading on virtual money than they would with real cash. This maverick behavior also seems to appear when they shift to live trading.

Overtrading – The thrill of trading the seemingly endless possibility to earn free money can cause many beginners working on a demo account to overtrade. However, this can be a very bad habit as this behavior can develop into a tendency to overtrade on the live market. You need to know quantity doesn't always trump quality.

Opening a Demo Account

When you decide that swing trading is for you then look online to find a broker and open an account. Of course, bear in mind everything that we have told you about finding a suitable broker that matches your needs should be relatively straightforward. It probably is best, but that is up to individuals to go for a broker with a good online demo system. The advantage of having a good demo system is that you can play about and test out all those tactics and metrics before you go too far into real-life trading.

Testing Stop-Loss

A "stop-loss" is a fixed price order that you make against a given trade that will trigger an automatic sell when the price hits that level. This mechanism can protect you in the event of a sudden fall in price perhaps through overnight market activity.

However, a stop-loss can also be used to lock-in profits in that scenario you would sell and take the profit when the price reached a desirable high level. Some traders adjust stock-loss or profit-take levels every day. They may even adjust what they call a "trailing stop" on their current positions. They do this by setting an order to trigger at, 10% or 15% below the price they paid for the stock. Of course, this requires that you continually evaluate what 10 or 15 percent is relative to your current stock value. This means that you will have to regularly check your stock position and calculate the new stop-loss position. Once you calculate the new stop-loss level, you will need to make an order to trigger at that level. This prevents losses. However, it can work the other way and lock-in profits. For example, if you bought a stock at $10 then set a stop loss at $15 and the stock goes to $20; that is a lot of unclaimed profit should the stock plummet. But here is the thing, once the price hits $15 it would be sold giving you $5 profit per share.

However, be warned as it can have unintentional results; for example, a stop-loss applied to some stocks may well back bounce quickly. Indeed a lot of investors have found themselves in the position where they have been "stopped out" of stock overnight. Only to see it bouncing right back up the very next day and reach a tremendous high. Of course, the opposite is also true that should your stock stop-loss order trigger after a 15% slide, and the stock keeps on tumbling, then it will save you a lot of money. But you will need to know the risks as well as the rewards when applying for stop-loss orders.

There are two types of order that a trader can initiate; a market order and a limit order. A market order will strive to buy the requested amount of stock at the best market price. A limit order, on the other hand, will only buy an available stock at a designated price.

Therefore we can use these orders to fulfill different tasks such as if we issue a "limit order" which has the same mechanics as a stop-loss order but is used on the upside. For example, you may want to buy Facebook stock, but currently, it is too expensive, so you are waiting for it to drop in price. In this scenario, you could place a limit order that tells the market that you're willing to buy stock but at only this price. Moreover, you can also use limit orders when transacting a sale. For example let us say that shares in a company are currently trending downwards and trading at $290, but $300 is your break-even price. It would be good to have an order that triggers a sale at $290 to limit your losses.

Now many people will say why sell at less than you bought for? And many professional traders do set a limit order and then steadfastly refuse to budge from it. However, if you contemplate the risk, you will see that if you refuse to sell at $290, the stock could backslide to $280 or continue to plunge into deeper losses. But there is also the thing it might rebound to $300 before it breaks out and hits $500. On the buying side, if you refuse to any pay more than $10 for a stock you are not convinced about as it is currently trading low, then you too can be caught out. For you could miss the opportunity to ride the wave when it goes up to $11 and then rises to $12 and then $14 and then $15, by that time you might feel $10 was in hindsight a very good price.

Summary

In this chapter, I shared with you the complexity of swing trading – or indeed any type of trading; it is not as easy as may seem. Protecting your capital is paramount, but there can be opportunity risks where you don't take the right trade at the right time. This is where diligent research comes into play and puts you on the right side of the deal. Do not gamble always go with the market flow. Always secure your potential losses and lock-in unclaimed profits in volatile markets. On the other hand don't be too conservative as opportunity-loss can be equally psychologically devastating.

Chapter 4 – Learning the Art of Swing Trading

In this chapter, we will show you how to best enter into swing trading. It is very easy, but that is where most beginners fail. Therefore, if you do not want to be among the long list of failed hobbyist traders then make sure you know what you are doing before you risk your money. We will provide you with good advice on a safe starting point that will help you preserve your capital. We will show you how to hone your trading skills using a variety of techniques to get on the right side of the market before you risk your money.

Learning the Art or Science of Swing Trading

Now that you have decided to try out swing trading you will be glad to know that you can find your feet and learn the basic skills by using simulation trades based on live, real-world stock but using virtual money. Many brokerages offer this service where you can safely learn in a virtual environment. The importance of using these simulations to learn, develop and practice your trading strategies cannot be overemphasized. You will however also need to undoubtedly develop your own trading strategy that suits your pocket and risk profile. After all, you don't want to be starting out trading using real money and no tested strategy. Therefore you will need first to learn how to swing trade and practice using the simulators to hone your skills and develop a strategy. A good way to develop those strategies and skills is to follow the methodologies of experienced swing traders and copy their typical approach to swing trading.

A day in the life of a Swing Trader

What you need to do before the Market opens is essential if you want to be successful. Professional swing trader will often rise and begin working long before the start of trading. Indeed it is often as early as 6.00 am if they can sleep through their trade notifications chiming on their phones. This is because it is very important for a trader to get an early impression of the prevailing conditions that have overnight affected slant of the day's market. Diligent traders will also need to check their existing positions' profitability and the effects on them from overnight trading which can be considerable. They will need to be on the look-out for new potential trades, and they may do this by making up a daily watch list.

Get an early impression of the Market

After you shake the sleep from your eyes and get some coffee the next task of the day is to fire up the computer and get an early impression of the market conditions. The most effective way to do this for beginners that are new to swing trading is via CNBC. There are also other media channels and websites as well as subscription services. However, most professionals are not interested in the actual details they just want to know what is better or worse about something such as is the SP500 up or down, or is the dollar trading higher than the Japanese yen? They don't get too embroiled in the detail they just want to know what is better today than yesterday or worse. The beginner should take that as a good tip. You should also keep to the traditional media sources before committing to a long term subscription service. Regardless of the source of the market intelligence, the beginner trader will have to keep an eye on three specific pointers:

1. The prevalent financial market condition, whether the market is bullish or bearish
2. Stock Sector Confidence, (what sectors are hot, what sectors are growing, what sectors are cold, etc.)
3. Current Economic Climate (based on the news on the economy, GDP earnings, Unemployment, etc.)

This crucial financial information can be determined via key economic reports as well as through published currency rates and inflation figures. Though that level of scrutiny is more for the professional analysts typically the beginners can get by just through scrutinizing the general trends in the key financial markets they will trade on. Remember that many professionals only judge news based on whether it is good or bad news they are not interested in the details. For example; are the stocks in their trading category or sector up or down?

Find Potential Trade Opportunities

Traders will always be on the look-out in the morning for new potential high-value trades. Typically, swing traders will first identify and buy stock with what is known as a fundamental catalyst. The experts will then manage or sell the stock on the basis of technical analysis. Now to understand what a fundamental catalyst is and how to find good fundamental catalysts we can use one of three methods:

1. Specialist opportunities: These are the opportunities that arise from unpredictable changes in a company's standing include going public, loss of a CEO, takeovers, mergers, and other similar major events that will be reported in the financial and business orientated media. These types of opportunities will indicate high risk and are not for the

2. beginner, well at least not without considerable simulated and paper trading experience. Nonetheless, for the
3. professionals, they often deliver large profits for those who have diligently researched each opportunity.
4. Focusing on a Specific Sector: Discovering this type of high performing stock is done by studying the business news and focusing on the updates that are relative to that sectors financial news. The objective of doing this fundamental analysis is that it gives you knowledge of which sectors are performing well. An interesting thing for you to note is that individual companies within a sector such as technology will perform alike as there are a lot of synergies. They will vary obviously in price index movement, but the trends will tend to be uniform across the entire sector. For example, you will be able to tell that the technology sector is trading hot by simply checking on the sector performance. This can be done by simply reading the news for mentions of the stock movement of the technology giants within the sector. If those giants are doing well and their stock is trending up, it is highly likely that all the other companies in that sector are undergoing a similar upward trend. Sector play will encourage the swing trader to buy into the sector sentiment rather than into

an individual company's stock. That way they are free from the risk of one single company

5. having at an ill-opportune moment and then they can ride the wave of the group's strength until the trend ultimately shows the signs of reversal or retracement.

6. Chart analysis or basic pattern recognition is also another method available to swing traders. Typically this sort of information is only available for heavily traded stocks. However, these types of plays require a trader to identify an entry point into the trade. However, if they are sufficiently talented and well informed, they can identify the breakouts which involve, buying after a drop in price and then selling again at the next peak level.

Draw up a Watch List

For you as a beginner swing trader to keep on top of your research and opportunities, you are best to take another leaf out of the professional's book and create a watch list. This is a list of potentially high-performing stocks that are trading which has caught your interest. Typically these will be a list of stocks that you have been advised on or have yourself detected by some basic fundamental analysis. These stocks will look like having the potential of being a good trade. A more detailed watch list which a professional might make up each day will typically contain a list of stocks with their entry prices and stop-loss prices that they want to keep an eye on.

Calculating the Existing Positions

Most importantly you must check up on the existing positions of your stock but do it on a regular basis not sporadically. The problem with random checks is that you can see losses or gains and then trade reactively trying to chase the losses. To do this, you will first need to check your current position then if everything is stable look to the overnight financial news to ensure that nothing untoward has happened, that may affect your stocks positions. This can easily be done by entering the assigned stock symbol into Google. If there is a significant change to your position, then you will have to see how it may affect your current trading strategy. Even if it doesn't, you may want to reconsider where to adjust your stop-loss or where to set your take-profit points.

After-Hours Market

Aftermarket hours is a dangerous time as it is the time when the rest of the world is trading. But it is the time where you can watch what is going on in real time, and if you can't sleep, you may want to do some of your own tradings. But even if you do not want to trade you may want to make adjustments to your position based on global market movements that offer opportunities for future trading. However, you only want to adjust profit-taking levels or adjust stop-loss levels upward to lock in profits. It is never a good idea to increase risk by moving a stop-loss down. After all, as we will see later, risk management is critical to long-term sustainability and financial survival. This period is for the swing trader the time for performance evaluation and a time to evaluate their position. Diligently evaluating your performance over a few days involves examining your analyzing of your trading activity and seeing where you went wrong or where you were successful and then determining the areas that need some improvement. By following this typical daily routine of an experienced swing trader, the one thing that stands out is just how important it is to follow a pre-market routine diligently. The researched and analysis performed on the previous day's trading and the intelligence gathered is critical to successful swing trading. After all, you have the advantage of holding a position for several days so this time should be spent finding trading opportunities and planning the day's trading strategy. Nonetheless, the market hours are the time spent trading except for adjusting risk or profit taking positions. Certainly, they should not be used for reactively devising any new strategies. Aftermarket time should be a time to review your short term trades and assess their overall performance. By creating and following a daily trading routine this will improve your trading; also it only requires some dedication and planning and really when we consider how much of your money is at stake is that so difficult.

Summary

In this chapter, we have looked at what you need to do to become a swing trader by describing a typical working day. We have also introduced you to the actual art and science involved as it takes a lot of research, analysis, and good judgment. However, even with those attributes, we will still need good preparation pre-market and performance monitoring post-market.

Chapter 5 - The Art of Selling Short

From the time you start trading the consensus of sage advice that you will hear is buy low and sell high. It is common sense really, but the problem is how do you make a profit in a bear market when prices are falling? In this chapter, we will reveal a very cunning trick that professional traders use to take advantage of the reverse swing. It may seem to be counter-intuitive and very strange at first but once you think it through it does make sense.

What is selling short all about?

When beginners first consider trading they intuitively think only about taking a long position where they will buy a stock that they believe will trade at a higher price at a future time. They see their profit coming from them buying low and selling high with the stock moving in an upwards trajectory. Now that is fine in a bull market where stocks are all trending in an upwards direction. But what do you do when there is a significant bear market where prices are falling and prices trending in a downward direction? The answer is as we have mentioned previously that you take a short position. Though it is not intuitive, you can profit from the decline in the price of a stock, but there are considerable risks that you need to be aware of. When you are short selling, you need to know what you are doing before you make any transactions as the mechanics are quite different from grasping initially, and the risks are high. So before you even think about trading short; practice, make sure you know that the important technical analysis techniques will often need to be reversed. But even before you start working on the simulator let us have a brief run through of what short selling is about.

Defining a short position

The short-seller definition is a trader involved in short selling that is taking up a position where he is going to sell a stock that he believes will fall in value. Now you might, as most beginners do, wonder how he can profit from doing that. However, there is an important caveat in that a short seller does not own the stock before he sells it. That is the bit that normally confuses the inexperienced trader. But the fact is that when you short sell you are selling borrowed stock – stock somebody else owns.

What happens is that you as the short seller borrow the stock you wish to sell short from someone who already owns it. Then you short sell the stock and are now banking that the stock value will fall in value once you have sold it. At a later period, you buy back the stock that you shorted at a lower price. Then you can subsequently return the borrowed stock to the owner to close out the loan and make a profit. If the market has behaved as you predicted and the stock has fallen into the price you can buy the stock back for less than you received for selling it. The difference is your profit.

What this technique allows is for traders to profit during the times of bear markets and falling stock prices. Interestingly, the principles of trading remain "Buy low, sell high." The mantra is valid whether you are short selling or going long. The fundamental difference is simply that with a short sale the stock is sold first and bought later.

But there are some caveats that we need to be aware of when selling short. The first and most important are that you trade with borrowed stock. But where do you get this borrowed stock from? Well, it is supplied by your broker, but to do this, you will have to open a margin account with them. Therefore, we can see that short selling is a margin transaction. A margin account allows you to use your stocks as collateral to borrow money from your broker. However, in this case, you want to borrow stock and the dealer doesn't carry stock so where do they get the stock from? The way it works is that when you open a margin account, you must sign a hypothecation / re-hypothecation agreement. This is a legal agreement that says you will pledge your stocks as collateral against your loan. But the re-hypothecation agreement allows your broker to loan your stocks to a bank, or other customers! Hence the broker can borrow stock from another customer more often than not without them even knowing about it as it's all done transparently in the background.

How to short sell

As we have just seen short selling differs from the traditional 2-party share purchase as it involves three; people the original owner, the short seller and the new buyer. The way it works is that when you wish to short sell, you will borrow shares via the broker from the actual owner, and immediately sell them to any willing buyer. To close out the short sale transaction, you must then buy back on the open market the same amount of shares as you sold earlier. The broker can return them to the original owner, and you retain the profit.

Therefore, before you can even think about selling short, you will first have to set up a margin account with your broker. However, you must understand that to take a margin account you are potentially getting yourself into debt. A margin account uses the value of your portfolio as collateral against any borrowed stock or loan. A rule of thumb is that there is a 2:1 ratio whereby the value of your portfolio must equal a minimum of 50% of the size of the short sale transaction. In practice, this means if you have a current portfolio worth

$1,000 in your margin account you can borrow $2,000 of stock to sell short.

That's the theory, and in practice, it is relatively straightforward. To sell a stock short, you must first borrow stock. Therefore to initiate a short sale, you contact your broker or trading platform and ask to sell short a specific number of shares of your selected stock. Then, your broker will need to verify that the shares are available and your credit limit meets the sales value.

If another customer of the broker holds sufficient stock the brokerage borrows the shares and sells them in the open market. The broker then puts the proceeds of the sale into your margin account. To close out your short sale, tell your broker that you want to purchase the same amount of shares that you shorted. Your broker will then purchase the shares using the funds in your margin account, and return the shares and close out the short sale transaction.

However, there are things to be aware of such as that the time your short sale is outstanding, you will be charged interest against the value of the short position. In addition, should the shorted stock go up in price, or the value of your portfolio falls below the maintenance level, which may be as much as 30% of the value of the short transaction, you will need to address the issue by topping up your margin account. If you can't do that, then you will have to buy back the stock you borrowed to close the deal perhaps at a significant loss.

As strange as short selling must seem to a beginner it is a perfectly valid and legal method of trading. It may seem counter-intuitive as surely short selling stock would accelerate a downturn and amplify pessimism in the stock leading to a crash. So why would anyone want to lend you their stock so that you could effectively devalue it and that is perfectly true? That is why there is a rule called the Up-Tick rule which determines that to sell your stock short the transaction before your short sale must have been executed at a higher price than the transaction before it. In other words, the transaction before your short sale must be an uptick. This effectively prevents short selling on a downward trajectory which protects the stock from free fall due to excessive short selling.

Why short sell?

Opportunism and portfolio protection are the two most common motivators for short selling, and both have their virtues. For example, if opportunism is the reason this will be because a trader believes that a stock is being vastly overvalued and hyped beyond reason. As a result, they are confident in their belief that the stock price will eventually fall to a realistic level. This is when they believe reality replaces the hype in the market. In this scenario, a short sale is a good strategy as it provides the opportunity to profit from the overpriced stock.

However, short sales have another strategic purpose as they are also used to protect an investor's portfolio against a market downturn. In this case, a trader may wish to use strategic shorting stocks if they predict a sharp fall in the market across all sectors. The way this works is that the trader will look for stock opportunities that are again overvalued and riding a wave of optimism. However, they believe that should market sentiments suddenly shift from overly optimistic to pessimistic it will be these stocks that will fall sharpest. By strategically short selling on those stocks the profits made from short selling the stock helps offset losses across the rest of the portfolio.

Now that we have covered a lot of the background of stock trading and some specifics about swing trading it is time to delve into the theory of fundamentals analysis. This might seem boring but understanding the fundamentals of stock trading can be the difference between being a successful swing trader and another victim.

Summary

Any sort of trading on financial securities is high risk but for the beginner going short is very risky. The problem is that once you move into a margin account, you are effectively trading on borrowed money – this could well accelerate your wins, but it is just as likely to wipe you out. Short trading is very profitable because it is high risk, but you must practice and be sure of what you are doing and be aware of the debt you are taking on board. Nonetheless, if you do learn the techniques and are comfortable short trading after a lot of practice, then it means you can play both sides of a market.

Chapter 6 - The Basics of Fundamentals Analysis

A very interesting question that many beginners ask is how do you find profitable stock? In this chapter, we will examine the methods and processes that professional institutional traders use to do just that. We will look into a technique called Fundamental Analysis, which is basically doing diligent research on the company that owns the stock or should you be trading currency on Forex on the relative economic results of the respective countries. However, you will learn many useful tips on how to evaluate a company's current financial health.

An introduction to Fundamental Analysis

Earlier we mentioned that the institutional traders and more experienced retail traders would enter into a trade based upon good fundamental catalysts which are strong indicators of the healthy financial prospects of a company. As to what makes for great growth potential in a company's stock is down to the fundamentals of the company's financial strength but that poses us with a few initial problems such as:

- How can we tell if the company will stay ahead of its competitors and maintain a dominant market position?

- How do we determine if it is in a position to grow its market share?
- How can we determine if the company's stock value will grow?
- How do we get an edge over our competitors by identifying these companies?

Unfortunately, no magic-bullet variable allows us to pick successful stocks—such as the traditional metrics of price-earnings ratio or price-to-cash-flow ratio. The harsh reality is we need to use a combination of fundamental variables in our research if we are to find these illusive high-earning stocks. This is also why brokerages charge so much for research.

Positive Earnings Revisions

One very important fundamental variable is a positive earnings revision. This comes about when market analysts who are typically cautious people decide that a company is performing better than they predicted. However when market analysts do upgrade a company's earnings forecasts they do so pretty reluctantly - after all, no-one likes to have to admit they got it wrong - so they still tend to stay on the conservative side. In which case, you can expect the actual real earnings to beat even the revised forecast.

Positive Earnings Adjustments

The second fundamental variable is earnings adjustments as once a company exceeds the market analysts' forecasts they tend to keep doing so. Therefore we need to look for stock that has really taken the analysts by surprise and comfortably beaten the forecasts.

Sales Growth

This is a far more intuitive variable because top line income is a great indicator of how well a company is doing and is hard to manipulate. Sales growth shows how a company is doing year-on-year, so all you need to do here is to compare the current quarter's sales from the same quarter for the prior year and compare the respective increases.

What you are looking for here is figures that show year-over-year sales increases of 20% or more as this indicates a company with good growth potential and a product that is in demand.

Reducing Operational Costs

Another good metric to a healthy company is if its operating margin is increasing this is referred to as Operational Growth Margin. This variable is determined simply by taking the operating income left after all operational expenses have been deducted divided by net sales. We then look at whether this percentage margin is contracting or growing year over year.

What you are looking for is a company that has an increased operating margin because this means they have either managed to cut operational costs – reduced employee headcount introduced automation, etc., or increased sales margins. The latter is indicative of a strong product and market position as it can sustain sales despite higher pricing.

Strong Cash Flow

Cash flow is simply how much free cash a company is holding. It is the amount of non-committed cash available to the company after paying all the costs and expenses. It is often the best indicator of a company's financial health. What you are looking for here is a company with significant free cash that can fund growth by developing new products. A company with no free cash to hand will struggle to keep the lights on if it's spending all of its income and probably more.

Earnings Growth

This simple measurement is usually measured in terms of earnings per share, which is just the company's earnings divided by the number of shares they have outstanding. However, this metric is the way we determine the companies that are earning more year-over-year. The way you can find out is by comparing the share earnings per quarter to see how they are increasing.

Earnings Momentum

This variable measures the growth of earnings year-over-year. This is one of the important variables as earnings momentum is one of the biggest driving forces behind stock prices during a bull market.

Return on Equity

Return on equity is the variable you use to measure corporate profitability. It's calculated by dividing the earnings per share by the equity (book value) per share. You are looking here for a high number that shows the company is profitable.

Companies that hold good market positions within their respective sectors tend to have very large returns on the equity invested. Also, companies that have a very high return on equity are more likely to be cash rich. But we can only compare returns on equity among companies in the same sector and not against other sectors – for example; we cannot compare banking with technology.

Concentrating on the Numbers

All of the indicators that we have just discussed are good measures of the financial health of a company. A company that scores well across all of these variables is likely to have all the characteristics of a company that can grow and increases its profitability and its stock value.

The importance of using all of the above variables is that it gives you a better chance of finding those elusive companies with great prospects. This can give you an edge over other traders who are sticking to 2 variables, and it also helps take the guesswork out of picking those high-performing stocks.

Nonetheless, for most beginners and even experienced professionals doing all that fundamental research to find the valuation of a company is very tedious. It's not as easy as it often requires reading several years of a company's financial statements such as their annual accounts, balance sheets, profit and loss, cash-flow, and income statements, etc.

However, the good news is that most of this information can be deduced using a few financial ratios which are readily available. Using these indicators, you can make informed choices about the best companies to invest in. On the other hand, you could use them in your fundamental analysis to compare the financial position of companies in the same sector.

Earnings per Share (EPS):

This key ratio is really important to understand as EPS is a company's last year's profit divided by the shares issued to the market. As a trader, you are looking for a company with stock trading at a higher EPS as this is a good indicator that the company is making a profit. With that in mind, evaluate its EPS over the last few years for if it has growing EPS, then that's even better. However, beware of companies where the EPS is falling or appears to be up or down over that same period.

Price to Earnings Ratio (P/E)

Whenever fundamentals are discussed this vector will come to the fore as it is the professional traders' favorite indicator. As a good rule of thumb, this is the value of the stock that you will be buying, so it is better to go for a low P/E ratio as a high P/E indicates overpriced stock. However, P/E is specific to a trading sector so is not comparable across different sectors (Technology, Energy, etc.)

A simple way to determine the best price of the shares is to consult a price line chart and compare the current closing stock price against previous closing prices. If you follow this method, you are using what is known as trailing EPS, which is based on the earnings per share over the last 12 months. There is also Forward EPS which is based on forecasted earnings per share. Trailing EPS is more objective and is based upon real historical data whereas Forward EPS is based on subjective projections.

Price to Book Ratio (P/B)

This metric is used to evaluate how much shareholders are paying for the net assets of a company. Generally, a lower P/B ratio may indicate that the stock is undervalued, but again this is not comparable across sectors.

Debt to Equity Ratio

The debt-to-equity is a measure of the relationship between what has been borrowed; typically debt and the amount of money invested by shareholders. Generally, as a company's ratio of debt-to-equity increases, it indicates a higher risk investment. On the other hand, if a company has a lower debt-to-equity ratio, it may indicate that the company is relying on less debt and has more investor confidence.

As a general rule, companies with a debt-to-equity ratio greater than 1 are considered to be higher risk and should be avoided.

Return on Equity (ROE)

The metric of Return on Equity (ROE) is based on the amount of net income the company returns as a percentage of shareholders investment. ROE is a good indicator of how well a company is performing and providing shareholders with a positive return on their investment.

Always try and check back over a few years as an increasing ROE is a very positive sign as is an ROI that is greater than 20%.

Price to Sales Ratio (P/S)

This is a very important indicator as it measures the price of a company's stock against its 12-month sales. The P/S ratio is very similar to the P/E ratio.

However, raking the top line sales figures as immutable is a good thing as other figures in the accounts can be heavily manipulated by moving dollars around. Therefore the ratio of profits to sales is useful because sales figures are considered to be relatively reliable and not easily manipulated using creative accounting techniques that bend the rules.

Current Ratio

This is another key financial ratio for evaluating a company's financial health by providing a clear indicator of its liquidity. The Current Ratio measures the difference between the current assets at hand that is available to cover current liabilities. This ratio reveals whether a company has the current ability to cover its short-term liabilities its debt against its short-term assets. You should consider that a positive sign is if the ratio is over 1 as this means the company has more short-term assets than short-term debts. On the other hand, if the current ratio is less than 1. then the company could be in a weak financial position as it is not in a position to cover its short-term liabilities.

As a general rule consider investing in a company that has a CR greater than 1 and avoid those with less than 1.

Summary

In this chapter, I showed you the necessary tools which you will need to evaluate a company's financial health. There is no better way to determine the relative value of stock than to compare it to the company's present financial position. Remember that markets are volatile; just this month in early 2019 Apple announced a forecast of a dip in profits of $55 billion due to the trade spat between the USA and China. The profound thing to take from this is even technology giants like Apple are vulnerable to single events so do your fundamental research.

Chapter 7 - The Basics of Technical Analysis

The experts say that it is based upon fundamental catalysts – things that excite you about a company's stock – that gets you into a trade, but it is a technical analysis that manages and keeps you profitable and also lets you safely exit a trade. Therefore in this chapter, we will go into the technical details of price and performance analysis. It might be terribly boring as it is hugely technical, but it can save you a lot of money.

An important thing for beginners to understand is that it is fundamental analysis – covered in the last chapter – that gets you into a trade, but its technical analysis that helps gets you out of it. Many beginners will make the mistake of believing that they don't need to understand either fundamental analysis or technical analysis because their broker or a subscription service provides them with all the market intelligence that they need with the click of a mouse; for many beginners that is a perfectly good solution. The problem is that you really do need to understand what they are telling you. If not you are just blindly following their lead and remember it is your money that will be lost not theirs. Of course, there are brilliant tools and online forums and services freely available that will do the majority of the heavy lifting for you and beginners should use these tools. But if you don't at least have a rudimentary understanding of how these tools make their decisions you could find yourself cleaned out in the first few months of trading. Therefore it is advisable to at least gain an elementary competence in understanding the science of technical analysis.

What is Technical Analysis?

The huge players in the stock markets around the world spend fortunes in research and technology to give them even the slimmest of advantages over their competition. They develop algorithms that take the decision making out of the hands of a trader or analyst. These mathematical equations can crunch through vast quantities of data faster than any human possibly can and trade at lightning speed. Similarly, even the low-end software available to beginners can analyze a stock's performance quicker and more reliably than a professional can – but they all work on the same core principles of technical analysis. Moreover, they are using the same freely available data which is typically the last days trading figures versus historical trading data.

Most technical analysis is based upon pattern recognition which is a particular strength of machine learning and AI which is why these technologies have come to the fore in high intensity and day trading whereby decisions must be made extremely quickly. However, in the less frantic world of swing trading, we can identify and analyze many of these patterns for ourselves.

DIY Pattern Recognition

Most beginners will start off using software or a subscription service to identify and select appropriate stock on which to trade. The beginner then doesn't need to know all the criteria that the software uses to determine what is and what isn't considered to be a good trade prospect. However, it is certainly beneficial to understand the basis for these automated decisions, and that requires having a rudimentary understanding of the different key variables the algorithms take into consideration.

A good place to start is in initially selecting a potential batch of stock for swing trading, and this should be done in the pre-trading period using a simulator. Even if you are trading live with your own money, this does not require the aid of software as the first general criteria are that beginners should restrict their selections to stocks that are at least $12 in price and have an average (20-day) daily volume of at least 500,000 shares. This is simply because the price is low enough to keep out the institutional investors as it's not worth their while. However, the price and volume are sufficiently high to keep out the market makers who can make it easier to manipulate low price, low volume stocks.

Furthermore, if we are interested in long swings, we should try and identify stocks that are moving in an upward direction. However, this is not as easy as it might seem so we will use some proven techniques to identify the indicators for such behavior. As a beginner, we can adopt the simplest indicators for trend analysis. We covered this earlier in the book, and it is quite simple as you compare the rising or falling stock over a given period. If it is a bull market, you can expect the stock to lift. On the other hand, if it's a bear market then as a beginner, you will avoid it like the plague.

The first and often most successful strategy is to consider the trend lines; whether the stock price is it going upwards or downwards over a specific period. One of the most powerful tools in the beginner's toolbox is trend-line analysis.

Trend line Analysis

A trend line is a historical stock price representation of past market movement sustained over a specific trading time frame. A trend may be either up, down or sideways. However, these trends do tend to persist so will likely last for weeks. Hence, they are clear indicators of the direction the stock price is moving. However, as we discussed earlier, there is within this primary trend regular minor interruptions called pullbacks. These are a variety of short-term blips that behave against the general trend. These blips can appear at any time and last for days or even persist for weeks, but they are valuable entry points into a trade.

An uptrend can be described as being a series of higher highs, and higher lows as the trend are upwards. Similarly, the reverse is true for a downward trend. It is often helpful when looking at a stock price line to label the peaks and valleys so that you can visually identify them using a "P" and a "V." This is also a good place to start when analyzing a chart as these peaks and valleys are not just trend indicators they are also indicators of support and resistance points for the stock, which we will discuss later. When labeling the peaks and valleys try to catch major swings and don't bother with the many small blips. By labeling the chart with the major peaks and valleys, it allows you to spot a trend as it develops. It also clearly illustrates when the trend might quickly change direction. Spotting this type of trend reversals is crucial to successful trading. It is critical to recognize these early warning signs of a trend reversal because they provide optimal entry and exit points in the trade. Doing a trend analysis by just using a chart may be simplistic, but many highly successful traders swear by it. These are rules that you should use every time. If you draw a trend-line on a chart, they are vital for keeping you on both the right side of that trade but also the market. However, you must realize that you should never fight against the market. A very effective swing trade strategy that a beginner should adhere to is the mantra; buy on the break of the down-pull and take your profits at the break of the up-pull. It is as simple as that; it is common sense but infuriatingly difficult to do.

Uncover the Support and Resistance Levels

When we watch stock fluctuate against the price we will often witness a strange occurrence where the stock falls only to a certain limit where it seemingly supported for some time. Similarly, we also see the stock rising that seems to appear to be breaking through the upper price barriers only to be rebuffed. As a result, the stock prices oscillate between the lower support price and the glass ceiling higher resistance price. Therefore we can consider a support level to be the level where the price tends to find support as it falls and subsequently bottoms out. This is where the price is likely to halt its descent and bounce and recover rather than fall through that support level. However, if the price does breach this level, it is almost certainly going to plummet until it meets another lower down support level.

A resistance level, on the other hand, is the opposite of a support level as it provides a blocking point where the price tends to find it difficult to break out off. This means that any optimistic price rises are more likely to "bounce" off this ceiling level rather than break through it. However, if there are sufficient momentum and the price breaches this level it is likely to continue rising until meeting another resistance level further up.

Strangely the roles are reversed once there has been a breakthrough and resistance become support and vice versa. The support and resistance levels can be identified with trend lines (technical analysis). The more frequent a support/resistance level is "tested," i.e., it is touched and bounced off by a price level the more significance is given to that specific level.

If however, a stock breaks past a support price level, that support level will often become the new resistance level. The opposite is also true; if price breaks a resistance level, it often finds support at that level in the future.

Fibonacci

The Fibonacci retracement pattern is often shown on charts as it can be helpful to traders identifying support and resistance levels. It is also useful in identifying possible reversal levels as stocks tend to repeat movements within a trend before reversing again. The technique works by drawing horizontal lines at the Fibonacci ratios of 23.6%, 38.2% and 61.8% across the stock chart and these visually demonstrate some likely support and resistance levels but also reveal potential reversal levels. You may find that some charts will highlight the 50% level as well, but that is not part of the Fibonacci pattern instead it is included because stocks do tend to gravitate back to the midway point. Unfortunately, it's not as simple as just trending or we would all be millionaires. Stocks shift irrationally. This is where support and resistance come into play. As we have just witnessed we see support and resistance where you see prices fall and rise, but they meet barriers that either supports them or act as a glass ceiling.

Trendlines, which we have already discussed and support/resistance levels are perhaps the two most important tools for analyzing a chart by a beginner. Nonetheless, we must understand both these concepts in great detail if we wish to be a successful swing trader. Understanding both the principles will provide a strong foundation in technical analysis that helps you improve your own ability to become a successful trader.

Reading Charts

Charts are the favored way for swing traders to analyses the technical data available to them about the position of a stock. You should search for highly visible chart patterns along the price lines such as rectangles, flags, pennants, heads, and shoulders as well as triangles. However to make sense of these charts we need to have a basic understanding of how to read them. Charts have some esoteric symbols and devices that are used to convey information. Hence to get the most out of reading these charts, we must understand the information that these symbols contain. Some like the Japanese Candle are simple visual representation; others though will require some calculation on your part.

Candlesticks

Candlesticks are a symbol on a price line chart that provides a lot of very important information. However, they also act as warning beacons that will inform you when a trend is about to change. You can think of them as a notification pop-up that gives you a warning about an impending change in market direction. You need to pay attention to them and heed their warning.

Candlestick charts use a device called a Japanese Candle to visually display the open, high, low, and closing prices. It uses an object similar to a standard bar chart that has two points that represent wicks at either end of the candle. The lower wick of the candle represents the lowest price while the top wick represents the highest price. The bottom and top of the Candlestick body represent the opening and closing prices respectively. The length of the Candlestick visually demonstrates the variance between the opening and closing prices. Candlestick charts are a quick way of looking at price movement, and they don't involve any calculations.

Some traders only use candlesticks when analyzing a chart, but it is best to use them along with other technical analysis tools like trendlines, support, and resistance, as well as your basic pattern recognition. Using multiple indicators often helps in detecting emerging, or illusive trends especially as they are not initially visible. Another great way to detect long term trends is to use Simple Moving Averages.

Simple Moving Average (SMA)

When contemplating an SMA, we will typically focus on three moving averages based on 10, 20, and 50 days. All moving averages smooth price movement and makes it easier to identify trends. The way it works is that it is simply the average closing price for a particular number of days. But it is also a moving average because, on every new day, the current day's price will be added to the average while the oldest price is dropped. This means that it is a good method for identifying trends as each calculation is based on the addition of the previous day's closing price. Moreover, it also provides a benchmark and a way of knowing how the stock's closing price yesterday relates to the moving averages of the last 10, 20, or 50 days.

What we need to look out for are the two key indicators that a stock is in the uptrend are:

- Today's closing price is both above the 10 day and 20 day moving averages.
- The 10 days moving average is over the 20 days moving average.

However, we are also looking for an entry point when looking for a long swing so that we can buy at a favorable price. Therefore, we would like to identify stocks that are experiencing a temporary pullback. If we can identify a pullback, we can perhaps buy at the lowest price. To identify a 3-day pullback, we need to compare the following indicators.

- The high price today is lower than yesterday's high
- The high from yesterday is lower than the high the day before

An uptrend will consist of higher highs and higher lows, but sometimes you get a lower high in an uptrend, so does that signify that the uptrend is about to change? Well just because you get a lower high and a lower low in an uptrend doesn't necessarily mean the general trend is over. This why we use the technique of Moving Averages as it will smooth out the anomalies in the charts over a longer timeframe.

For example, if you plot the Moving Average on a price line chart, you will see that if the current price is above the 20-day MA and the MA is over the period following a higher trajectory, then the market is most likely in a long-term uptrend. Also if the price is above the 20-day MA, and the MA is also pointing upwards, then the market is also likely to be in a short-term uptrend.

As a result of this, we can use the MA to measure the strength of the trend by looking at the steepness of the MA's line. So we can see that the steeper the gradient of the MA lines the stronger the trend, the flatter the MA, the weaker the trend.

This is where we come to the thorny question of how long an MA timeline we should consider. The simple answer is that using an MA as an indicator can help surface trends. But if you are trying to find and trade long-term trends then using a 20-day MA will be more productive. On the other hand, if you are trying to locate short-term trends then a much shorter 10 EMA would be preferable. But most people go between a 20 & 50 EMA to define the area of value.

A short-term MA such as a 5-day EMA will let you locate and benefit from short-term trends whereas a long-term MA such as a 20-day EMA will let you discover and benefit from long-term trends.

If you want to go long, you'd want to play along with the strongest trend in the market. If you want to go short, you would want to short the weakest trend in the market. Using MA allows you to discover the best trends in the market and then you will have a higher probability of putting yourself on the right side of that trend.

There are various methods to determine the relative strength of trends in the market. One of the easiest way is to use MA.

Step 1: choose the markets which are within the same sector.

Step 2: Plan the 20 & 50 EMA on your chart. Some charts may already include them.

Step 3: Compare the steepness of MA. The steeper it is the weaker or stronger the market.

Volume

In Technical Analysis a very important but basic component when evaluating the strength of the market position is volume. This is because volume provides clues as to the intensity of a given price move as it represents the total number of shares traded during a given timeframe (e.g., hour, day, week, month, etc.).

High volume levels are characteristic of high market optimism as there's a strong consensus that prices will rise. High volume levels also are very common at the beginning of new trends such as when prices break out of a trading range, i.e., when these burst through a resistance level. On the other hand, high trading volumes can also be a sign of panic selling just before the market bottoms. Either way examining volume can help us determine the strength of an existing trend.

Equivolume

This is another beneficial indicator as it displays the correlation between price and volume should one exist. Equivolume does this for us as it displays prices in a manner that illustrates the relationship between price and volume in one graphical device. Equivolume uses a similar object as a bar chart to candlestick to show the high price at the top line of the box and the low price at the bottom line. However, the unique aspect of equivolume is that it is the width of the box that represents the amount of volume for the period.

The shape of each Equivolume box represents the supply and demand for that specific stock visually. If the equivolume box is short and wide, this indicates a heavy volume of trading accompanied by small changes in price. On the other hand, a configuration that is tall and narrow indicates light volume accompanied with large changes in price. One special type of equivolume box configuration is called a "power box," and this has both exaggerated height and width. Power boxes provide excellent confirmation of a breakout. We must always look at volume regarding its relationship with price movement, and by doing so, we can make some informed decisions such as:

- Above average volume but with little significant price movement is an indication of a trend reversal

- Above average volume after a huge advance or decline is also a sign of a trend reversal

However, it is also true that the following conditions are also good indications of a trend persisting when there are;

- Above average volume but with significant price shift
- Above average volume with an indication of a successful breakout
- Below average volume with no or little significant price shift

Why we use Technical Analysis

A common belief amongst market traders is that the more skilled you are at technical and fundamental analysis, the more money you are going to make by trading stocks.

Technical analysis is the skill in interpreting a stock chart. The objective in technical analysis is all about using data to determine a stock's trend and finding the optimal entry and exit points of trade. Technical analysis is about helping you stay on the correct side of that trend. As a beginner in short-term swing trading, it is important that you don't overlook the basics. For example don't lose track of the analysis of trend lines, support/resistance, and volume, as well as the basic pattern recognition method but there are many other advanced techniques you might like to experiment with.

The stock market is so complex and hard to understand because there are at any time a myriad of buyers and sellers negotiating trades. The sheer volume and volatility make having a coherent understanding of how prices will shift and in which direction hard to comprehend. But the basic rules that govern the markets are very simple in that there are buyers and sellers. If there are more buyers than sellers, then the market price goes up. But on the contrary, if there are more sellers than buyers, then the market prices go down. There's nothing complicated or magical about this. It is how all markets and trade works. The problem is for swing traders; on the stock exchange, you are both a buyer and a seller dependent on your current position.

Therefore, we can see that it is the price at which a stock is offered which affect the trader's position whether to be a buyer or a seller. If a trader is trading long and the stock positions he is holding starts to decline, the trader will consider selling to close his position. Hence, because of the nature of your trade when you take a long position, you naturally become a potential seller. On the other hand, while you are holding short positions, you are looking for the price to drop so that you can become a potential buyer. Technical Analysis becomes invaluable because it casts light on the otherwise ambiguous position of the swing trader. This is because as the prices information about the condition of the stock is revealed, you can use your technical analysis techniques to determine what position to take – a buyer or a seller. Moreover, you can further take confidence in your decision by examining the data trail that is left on price changes due to buying and selling pressure and by the combination of price and volume. What you want to remember is that the huge institutional investors leave a heavy trail as they are making vast transactions in both volume and price. However, that level of trading has a major impact on the market that reveals their optimism or pessimism about the current state of the market. And that is important how you as a beginner will stay on the right side of the market as you strive to follow in the giant's footsteps.

Summary

Technical analysis is complex, but it is also hugely rewarding. If you learn even the basics, it will give you an edge on the market. However, as a beginner focus on trends and patterns as they are reliable indicators of a market's direction. Many experts use 20 or 30 metrics to evaluate a stock, but that is just overcomplicating things. As a beginner you should practice with all these indicators but until you can prove their worth in paper or demo practice, stick to the tried and tested indicators of trend lines, moving averages, trading volume, and candlesticks.

Chapter 8 - Designing a Swing Trade Strategy

In this chapter, we will address the most important issue with financial trading – having a strategy. The focus on this chapter is to stress just how important having a through-out strategy is too successful trading. A common cliché is that without a plan you are planning to fail and in swing trading that is probably true. Therefore you must decide what you want from your swing trading and have clear objectives. When we consider creating a swing training strategy, the first step should be to consider why we need a strategy. After all, we have learned all about how to select stock using fundamental analysis and how to enter and exit a trade using Technical Analysis. Also, we have a firm pre-market and after-market schedule of tasks that cater to research and performance analysis. The problem, however, is that without a strategy all that is merely going through the motions of being a swing trader. To be successful requires that you have a plan and have set ambitions, but achievable goals or targets. After all without challenging targets how will you know if you are successful? Sure you may be making money, but could you be making more? Indeed for the time and effort, you are putting in and the risk you are taking should you be making more?

Devising a Swing Trading Strategy

We can only answer those questions if we can gauge our performance against challenging targets. However, for those ambitious targets to be met will require a carefully thought out plan which you will stick too. After all, do we want to be starting the day frantically chasing ill thought out goals to chase profits? Some traders do enjoy working that way as they enjoy the thrill of pitting their skills and gut-feelings against the markets. But for a beginner changing tactics haphazardly to try and achieve vague or shifting goals especially if trying to make good losses is not a good approach. That only exacerbates the risk, and the risk is already high enough. What we need to do is to sit down and think carefully about setting ourselves challenges but achievable targets and a plan on how we will achieve them.

Setting Profit Targets

Setting realistic profit targets is a contentious area as everyone has different expectations and risk aversion levels. Everyone has to decide what kind of trader they want to be. For example, do you want to ride the wave of a winning streak and capture the big profits? Or will you be content with securing small profits that are consistently achievable with an emphasis on maximizing your winning percentages?

Unfortunately, it is highly unlikely that you can get both. What we do know is that statistically if you want to trade in stock that offers 3 to 1 or perhaps even 5 to 1 or even more on your risk, then you must expect your winning percentages to be low. But it is hugely important to understand that the market is not a bookmaker offering odds – you are the one that is setting those very subjective odds.

Bookmakers don't gamble - they balance their books

If you're content making small profits trading 1 for every 1 of risk, then winning percentages of 60-70%+ are obtainable. You should know from your practice trading either on paper or the simulators how well you have performed and what profit is realistic. That was the time and still is, to practice with virtual money and test out new tactics. So you should now be comfortable with the trading process and have an optimistic but realistic ideas of what you want to achieve from your trading. Now, all we need to do is figure out an optimal path - less effort and less risk - to achieve those goals. And that will be your swing trading strategy.

You will need a strategy – a basic set of rules - to achieve and maintain consistency. By trading within these rules, you can then document your results, verify performance, and identify what is and is not working.

Keep Basic Principles in Mind

As a basis for a generic swing trading strategy, it is a good foundation to build on the basic concepts. As a swing trader, you will be playing an active role in trading the markets where your planned holding position extends beyond a day. The goal as a swing trader is to profit from short-term movements in the marketplace. Moreover, your focus as a swing trader is to capture a single leg (swing) in a stock's trend before exiting. Fortunately, there are several tried and trusted swing trading strategies for identifying potential stock for profitable trading.

Trade - don't Guess!

Nonetheless, your trading strategy should not just be about identifying stock to trade or focused on making a profit it is also intended to mitigate risk and preserve your capital. Therefore due to the short time frame of swing trading, the primary decision-making process is to get in and out of market quickly, but this is nearly always based on market conditions. As a result, we need to work with those market conditions to find the ideal entry and exit points so that we can efficiently ride the wave of a stock's swing. But to do that we need to analyze technical market data to find those often repeatable patterns. As a beginner, we can use software or advice from brokers, or we could use basic technical analysis techniques such as trend lines to identify the peaks and valleys or support/resistance to keep us on the right side of the market.

By using these basic but highly effective technical analysis tools, we will better identify the ideal entry and exit point. It doesn't matter much on which method you choose so long as you stick with it. This doesn't mean you're stuck with it forever the whole point of a strategy provides goals and benchmarks to test other techniques against just not in live trading.

Go with the Flow

We have already seen that trading against the market direction is a very bad idea. So in our strategy, we want to confirm our direction, and the best way to do this is to follow the trends.
The definition of a trend:
Uptrend – consists of higher highs and lows

Downtrend – consists of lower highs and lows

Therefore, if you want to find the path of least resistance, look to the left of the price line and then follow the trend. A few pro tips
are that if the price is in an uptrend, you should go long but if the price is in a downtrend, you should go short.

Determine a set of methods and techniques

Another good strategy is to follow price movement patterns to identify whether a stock is trending or is range-bounded. Analyzing a timeline chart is a quick way to get visual confirmation of a trend – a movement from bottom left to top right – or a range-bounded stock – sideways with no clear winners or losers. There're lots of ways you can come up with a rules-based definition for classifying these price action states, some examples you might consider in addition to trend-lines and support/resistance are Moving Averages or using technical patterns and geometrical shapes.

It is well worth your while experimenting to find a method that you are comfortable with before persisting with it as part of the strategy. This is because identifying these types of market conditions is a big advantage for once a market is trending; it tends to want to persist in that state. The same applies to range-bound markets they can be highly resistant to change. What you will find is that most breakouts will fail; market environments are resistant to change so always seem to want to revert to the means.

At this point, we have only considered what tools we want to use or rather we are comfortable with, but we still need a strategy – a set of rules to constrain our trading behavior and exuberance. So, let's take a look at an example of a priceline trading strategy.

Develop Trading Tactics

Using your priceline observations to identify a viable trending stock, and leveraging what we know about trends being persistent, you could put together some basic rules to form a trading strategy for trading in a pullback within an uptrend:

- Only target stocks in uptrends and exclusively trade in that direction.
- Use a predefined stop loss to make sure you limit losses.
- Make sure to take partial profits at a rate of a 1.5X multiple of risk to prevent losing profit.
- Let the leftover half of the trade run, as long as the trend is willing to take it to maximize profit.

To translate those intents into actions, we could then define a set of rules as being:

- Wait for a close under the 20 period Moving Average (MA)
- Buy the first bar that closes back over the 20 MA and the prior day highs.
- Place a stop at 1 Average True Range (ATR) below entry price or below prior swing low.
- Take half of the trade-off at a 1.5X ATR multiple.
- Exit the leftover on a close below the previous three-day lows.

With this strategy, we have defined a set of rules that determine, an entry, profit-taking, and exit condition. Moreover, we also have included some risk management using an initial stop loss at 1 below the true range or below the prior swing low. ATR is a measure of volatility, so we are protecting ourselves from dropping below the average or below the prior swings low point.

Of course, this strategy will only work well under those strict uptrend conditions so will need to be thoroughly tested against a variety of stocks under different trending conditions and perhaps tweaked to suit. However, this is what is termed backtesting and should be done off-market by paper trading or using an online simulator. It cannot be stressed enough that experimentation and backtesting should always be done through paper trading or on the simulator.

So far, we have only touched on some of the common tools and practices that a beginner to swing trading should be comfortable with. There are many other technical analysis tools we discussed earlier that you might want to practice with during your paper trading or simulator sessions. By common consensus, most experienced traders recommend using the techniques we have outlined above such as trend lines and price movement as well as support and resistance in conjunction with other technical analysis tools. The belief is that once you start to get positive results from these different tools and techniques and they all converge and reinforce one another in pointing towards a reversal or a breakout, then you could be onto a winner.

Put risk into the mix

So far, we have looked at some ways of entry and exit for a specific market condition of stock on a persistent up-trend. But what about risk management and position sizing?

Risk management and position sizing are extremely important in trading. It may seem like a lot of common sense, rules, and principles but there are huge variations in traders' risk aversion, and the best-laid strategies can go horribly wrong in the hands of a reckless trader. Here are some quick risk management tips and general guidelines to consider.

- Always have a pre-determined exit strategy which is a price where you will exit the trade.
- Never risk more than 1% per trade.
- Never have more than 20% of your total capital in a single security.
- Always study the stock's volatility (true average range) over a longer period to get an idea of the volatility you'll be dealing with.

A final point when considering your swing strategy is to look at setting a risk/reward level that you are comfortable with. We discuss risk and reward in the following chapter.

Summary

Developing a strategy is very important as it focuses you on the objectives that you hope to achieve while at the same time it mitigates risk or the loss of your capital. Without a coherent strategy, you may as well be gambling. Therefore, spend time analyzing your tactics to see that they are appropriate for reaching your goals and practice them before you put them into a live trading environment.

Chapter 9 - Managing Risk

The theory that underpins all financial trading is that it is based on three human emotions of Greed, Hope and Fear. Therefore, we need to control our emotions, so they do not get in the way of successful trading. In this chapter, we will consider techniques that allow us to trade rationally so that we can at least contain our losses.

There are many views on risk management which is largely dependent on whether you are reading good practices or listening to trader folklore. Some traders are high risk tolerant whereas others are risk averse. Regardless of your risk appetite, you should make yourself aware of the risk management tools and best practices to protect your capital by minimizing your losses. In this section, we will look at key areas of risk management from both a theoretical and later on a practical, real-world perspective. The reason for this is because many of the risk management tools available to us work fine in theory, but we must be aware of their practical limitations in challenging market environments.

Proper Position Size

The most basic risk management strategy available to us all is simply to control the amount you lose on each trade. This is of course down to personal risk appetite, but the consensus among brokers and traders is that you should cap your risk at about 1% of your capital per trade. For beginners, even after extensive time spent paper trading or on simulations you still might want to go even lower, to begin with, a level at 0.3%. The reason some recommend this is that they will tell you that paper trading or using virtual money just isn't the same as the real thing. Trading with real money affects you differently psychologically and sometimes makes you trade irrationally. Hence they recommend lowering your position for at least the first six months to around 0.3% before moving up gradually to 0.5% then 0.7% before moving up to the 1% level. At the lower level of 0.3% means that if you have an $8,000 broker account you can lose $24, but at the recommended level for experienced traders of 1%, that means if you have an $8,000 broker account, you can lose up to $80 per trade.

Of course, for those who are risks tolerant risking 1% or less may seem like a trivially small amount that may well hinder their ability to purchase selected stocks. This is especially true if you have a large account and similarly large ambitions. However, you need to be aware that you can grow your capital quite quickly by keeping your risk to 1% per trade. This is because even when you have a losing streak of several trades in a row, the corresponding losses won't hurt you too much. On the other hand, that same losing streak on a 5% or 10%

could well clean your account out. Also, if you pick your stock and positions strategically, targeting low-profit high-percentage wins, then your wins are often bigger than your losses. In that case, even if you only win 40% or 50% of your trades, you are building up your trading capital. Subsequently, as your experience and your trading account grow then your percentage gains will translate into larger dollar amounts each month.

A critical element of trading success is taking the appropriate position size on every trade. Position size is how much shares you take on a stock trade. However, choosing the right position size should not be just some arbitrary figure, nor should it be related to your confidence in the stock you are trading nor even how convinced you are a trade will be profitable. Rather, the correct position size is determined by a simple mathematical formula. Using this dispassionate scientific approach helps control risk and maximizes returns on the risk that's taken.

Determining the proper position size requires three steps:

Determine Account Risk

Regardless if your account is large or small—$1000 or $500,000—a single trade shouldn't put more than 1% of your trading capital at risk. On an $8000 account, you should not risk more than $80 on a trade, if your account is $2,000 you can risk up to $20 per trade.

Determine Trade Risk

To determine your position's size, we must set a stop-loss level. A stop-loss is an order that closes out the trade to negate the trade thesis if the price moves against us. What that means is you will set a stop order level that is low enough that when triggered after it reaches a specific price will prevent your losses escalating. This order is placed at a logical spot which is out of range of normal market movements caused by volatility for example, but if hit perhaps erroneously it will at least let you know that you have misjudged the current direction of the market.

Therefore, you will need the trade risk to move onto the next step in determining proper position size. Assume you buy a stock at $9.50, and place a stop loss at $9.40. The trading risk is $0.10.

Determine Proper Position Size

You now have all the information you need to calculate the proper positions size. You know your account risk, and you know your trade risk. However, it's important to understand that trading risk will be different on each trade so it will need to be calculated per trade. Also, your account risk will change over time as your balance changes – hopefully, grows – so hence your position sizes will be different from one trade to another trade.

To calculate position size, use the following formula:
Account Risk ($) / Trade Risk ($) = Position size in shares
Assume you have an $8,000 account, which means you can risk $80 per trade (1%). You buy a stock at $100 and a place a stop loss at $98, making your trade risk $2.
Stocks: $80 / $2 = 40 shares.

40 shares are your ideal position size for this trade because based on your entry and stop loss you are risking exactly 1% of your account. The trade costs you 40 shares x $100 = $4,000. You have enough money in the account to make this trade, so leverage is not required.

The 3 step approach is a good quick method of determining your correct position for any trade. However, it does mean that you might contravene another trading maxim as we have in the example above by placing more than 20% of our capital in one security. So if we want to ensure that we also have correct placement as well as the diversity of stock we need another solution.

Therefore, if you don't want to put all your capital into only a few trades, you can take another approach. In this alternative method, you can divide the total sum held in your account by 10, thus putting 10% in each stock that you decide to trade. On an $8,000 account, you can put $800 into each stock. Let's assume you want to put 20% of your capital into each stock. On an $8,000 account, that means buying $1,600 worth of stock on each trade. On each position, you will still need to put a stop loss to control your risk. This approach is often a simpler method for many people to understand. Buy a fixed amount of stock on each trade, and then set the stop loss wherever it should be for that trade.

Risk Reward Strategies

The risk-reward indicator measures how much your potential reward will likely be for every dollar you risk. It is something that you must be aware off so that you know with each trade whether the rewards justify the risk. We can think of risk-reward as a simple ratio, so if you have a risk/reward ratio of 1:3, this means you're risking $1 to make $3 potentially.

If you have a risk/reward ratio of 1:5, it means you're risking $1 to make $5 potentially.

Now there is much debate about what is an acceptable risk-reward ratio as some traders will not go less than 1:3 and prefer even higher rewards like 1:5. On the other hand, many thrive on the high percentage successes with 1:2 or even 1:1. This ambiguity is also down to the fact that the risk-reward ratio is misunderstood and pretty meaningless on its own.

Traders will minimize their potential losses using stop-loss orders. This is when traders will hedge their bids on individual stocks and directly manage their loss positions with a risk/reward focus.

For example: Say you want to purchase 100 shares of ABC Company at $10 and you place a stop-loss order at $5 to ensure that your losses will not exceed $500. Now, lets us assume that you have a belief that the price of ABC will reach $20 in the next few months. In this case, you are risking a $5 bid to return a profit of $10 per share after closing the position. Since you stand to make a sizable profit against the amount that you have risked, you have a 1:2 risk/reward trade.

Now if we consider that you might like a more conservative position of 1:5 risk/reward for a specified investment then you can change the stop-loss order. You would do this to adjust the risk/reward ratio. In this example if you want to hold a position where it is at a 1:5 risk/reward required for your investment, you would need to set the stop-loss order at $8 instead of $5 – then you are risking $2 for every $10 or a 1:5 risk/reward.

A thing to note is that to come to the risk/reward profile of 1:5, you changed the prospective rewards. Your research will have let you know that the maximum upside was $20 that should have been based on your technical analysis and fundamental research.

Had you just picked that number of $20 just out of the air then the whole thing is meaningless, for you to find an acceptable risk/reward the prospective rewards must be based on the objective result from diligent research. Also, try to never find yourself in a situation where the risk/reward ratio changes against you and the prospective rewards no longer look like materializing.

The problem with the risk/reward ratio is that it is more useful to institutional traders rather than retail swing traders as its reward is based on rigorous and diligent research of the stock. These institutional traders are using the risk/reward more as a comparison against other trades to see where they can best invest their institutions capital or their client's money. Typically, they will not go near anything under 1:3 as it just isn't worth the risk but anything better is few and far between. However, for the independent retail trader, all of these risk/reward ratios are practically meaningless as they rarely will have the resources to perform or buy the hugely expensive research into one company's stock let alone many. Instead, they tend to use the risk part alone and use their own risk appetite to decide their own acceptable losses on the deal.

Trading with Profit Targets

Another way to manage risk is to trade with profit targets as the focus. You will still of course use stop orders to prevent things from going bad but now the focus of the deal shifts to the actual profits that can be realized. There are several pros and cons with profit targets such as:

Pros

- Failure to lock in gains before the market starts pulling back can be a huge problem as you're consistently going to lose your unrealized profits and in such a volatile market, profit targets become essential.
- By having an achievable goal, it reinforces positive feedback and feedback builds confidence.

Cons

- When you have a specific profit target in mind, you are binding yourself to that set price.
- This limits your upside because you're placing a cap on your potential profit.
- Trending trades are very likely to continue to run past the set profit target, and you will miss out

The problem with these is; which is a better type of question, and the answer is usually, well it depends. And that is the case here. It may seem crazy to set yourself a fixed exit profit target, and then bale out of the deal especially on an up-trending stock, but it is disciplined. You set a profit target for the deal, get what you want and get out of there by minimizing risk. For example, in many market environments that suffer high volatility, it is essential to have tight profit targets and lock-in any realized profits before the market turns and wipes them out.

One solution is to try a hybrid type methodology whereby you set profit margins and profit lock-ins but only partial profit targets rather than full exits. That way you will lock-in and remove the profits, reduce your risk but also remain in the trade albeit at a reduced presence.

Summary

The importance of risk management in any manner of trading in financial instruments cannot be overstated. It is imperative that you diligently act to preserve your capital at all times. Therefore, you should limit your exposure to no more than 1% of your trading account on any single trade. Of course, if you have only limited funds, this can make trading difficult, but at least with swing trading, you should be entering only a limited number of high-profit trades a month, so the ratio of transaction costs to profits is not as prohibitive as in day trading. In order to look after your money stick to correct position sizing and use stop orders and profit-locks that will minimize any potential losses or safeguard your profits respectively. Finally, try not to gamble and have a clear strategy in mind as well as a logical reason why you are trading that specific stock – it should be based on a combination of fundamental and technical analysis – and not pure guesswork.

Chapter 10 – Wrapping it all Up

In this book, we have looked at ways that a beginner can successfully enter into swing trading. We have covered many elementary things that you need to know such as how the stock market works and how trades are made through a brokerage. Later we described how you could safely get started using paper or demo account trading to learn and hone your skills and strategies. Nonetheless, it has not all been about the basic skills as we have covered all of the intermediary techniques that you will require to swing trade successfully. For instance, we have covered in detail how to conduct fundamental and technical analysis as well as how to use that knowledge to enter and exit trading positions optimally. Furthermore, we have explained strategy and the importance of developing your own coherent swing trading strategy and tactics. Finally, and most importantly we have given you precious advice on how to manage the risk and preserve your trading fund capital.

In this closing chapter, we would like to take the opportunity to pass on some best working tips from experienced swing traders that will help you on your journey to becoming as skilled and successful as they are.

13 Top Tips for successful trading

Swing trading is not a way to make easy money it is very difficult, but if you keep these objectives in mind you will be ahead of the market:
1. Trade on an Uptrend – this is a trend that is characterized by a series of higher highs and lows
2. If you are risk tolerant then trade on a downtrend – this is a trend that is characterized by a series of lower highs and lower lows
3. Try and find the path of least resistance – trade with the market – so look early on the price line and then follow the trend.
4. When the price is in an uptrend, bid long.
5. When the price is in a downtrend if you must then borrow stock to go short.
6. Support levels – look for a level where falling prices are stalling as this is a good entry point into a trade; also it is a good indicator that a stock price may well go higher
7. Resistance – look for a glass ceiling where prices seem to bounce off as this is a good indicator of market sentiment
8. High probability trading — try using pattern recognition techniques to discover patterns like pennants, flags, triangles, and rectangles to identify

well-known trading precursors these tend to act like omens that help you identify areas of potential value

9. There are 3 ways you can enter a trade after diligent fundamental analysis, and that is to use the most common way and enter during a pullback, or if you get lucky and can identify a breakout, or after a failed test against a current support\ resistance level.
10. There is one way to exit a trade confidently, and that is based on scientific data by using technical analysis
11. Only ever trade with money you're prepared to lose
12. Never chase losses that are known as the risk of ruin whereby losses will grow exponentially as you overtrade in hope trying to win big to claw back your losses
13. Understand and try to control the three emotions that underpin financial trading Fear, Greed and Hope

Summary

In this book, we have strived to help the beginner in safely entering the domain of swing trading, hence the emphasis on the hugely important area of risk as it is imperative that you protect your funds and don't trade in a cavalier fashion. There is a fine balance between ambitious trading and reckless trading so test this out on paper trading or using a demo account. Also understand that there's no such thing as free money as profits you make will be hard won on the back of hours of research and considerable stress. However, there is potential for you to make a profit if you follow the guidelines in this book and do not come consumed by greed, fear or hope. Analysis can always help you identify good trades, and if you play safe and stay on the right side of the market, then the risk is always manageable. So, don't be too alarmed for the information that we have summarized in this chapter will go a long way in protecting your capital and allowing you to trade safely. In conclusion, we have provided a beginner's charter of the best tips we have collected from many swing trading experts to help you in your trading - so pay attention to them, pay heed and keep on the right side of the market. If you can do that, we are sure that you will have a long and successful trading career – so good luck, good trading, and good profit!

Thank you!

Before you go, I just wanted to say thank you for purchasing my book.

You could have picked from dozens of other books on the same topic but you took a chance and chose this one.

So, a HUGE thanks to you for getting this book and for reading all the way to the end.

Now I wanted to ask you for a small favor. **Could you please consider posting a review on the platform? Reviews are one of the easiest ways to support the work of independent authors.**

This feedback will help me continue to write the type of books that will help you get the results you want. So if you enjoyed it, please let me know! (-:

www.ingramcontent.com/pod-product-compliance
Lightning Source LLC
Chambersburg PA
CBHW071716020426
42333CB00017B/2296